TRACK AND COPY

Exercises to improve focus and visual skills

Visual Treasure Chest

TRACK AND COPY
Exercises to improve focus and visual skills

Focusing is an essential cognitive skill that enables us to concentrate on a particular task or information while ignoring distractions. It involves selectively allocating our attention and effort towards a specific goal or objective, and it requires mental discipline and self-control. Focusing can be challenging, especially in today's world where we are constantly bombarded with information and distractions from various sources such as social media, emails, and notifications. Research has shown that practicing focusing skills can enhance our cognitive abilities, increase our productivity, and improve our overall well-being.

Visual skills are a set of abilities related to the processing and interpretation of visual information. Strong visual abilities are important for many everyday tasks, such as reading, writing, driving, playing sports, and navigating through the environment. Improving visual skills can be achieved through various methods, such as performing eye exercises, for example, tracking moving objects or focusing on objects at different distances, and engaging in activities that require hand-eye coordination, for instance, drawing or copying patterns.

Visual skills and focus are closely related because both involve the ability to concentrate and pay attention to visual information. Visual skills, such as visual tracking, visual perception, and visual memory, rely on the ability to focus on and process visual information. Similarly, focus is necessary for the brain to effectively use visual skills to interpret and make sense of visual information.

The aim of this book is to help readers improve their ability to focus and develop stronger visual skills. The workbook contains exercises at three different levels, each designed to challenge and improve the reader's visual skills and focus. The tasks involve tracking and copying a given pattern, which requires the reader to pay close attention to the details and use their visual skills to accurately reproduce the pattern. The exercises are structured in a way that gradually increases in difficulty as the reader progresses through the levels. The execution of every exercise requires more attention and concentration as the level increases, which helps to build and improve the reader's ability to focus.

This book can be a helpful resource for anyone looking to improve their focus and visual skills, regardless of age. It is also a useful tool for teachers, therapists, tutors, and parents who support patients or students in developing and mastering visual skills and focusing.

How to use this book?

1. Choose an exercise. You can select among tasks at three different levels of difficulty.

2. Begin with the dot that is marked. Track the pattern from dot to dot and copy it to the grid that is beside or on the next page. Focus and try to be accurate. You do not need to hurry.

3. Check your pattern for possible errors.

You can use a pencil or a pen. Avoid thick markers that could bleed through the page.

Additionally, for every level, you can create a pattern of your own. You will find empty grids at the end of this workbook.

Exercises list

Level easy

- **1-5** - 3x3 grids - 12 patterns on every page
- **6-10** - 4x4 grids - 9 patterns on every page

Level medium

- **11-17** - 6x6 grids - 3 paterns on every page
- **18-24** - 10x10 grids - 2 patterns on every page

Level hard

- **25-30** - 19x19 grids - one pattern on every page

Extra pages

- empty grids for every level of difficulty

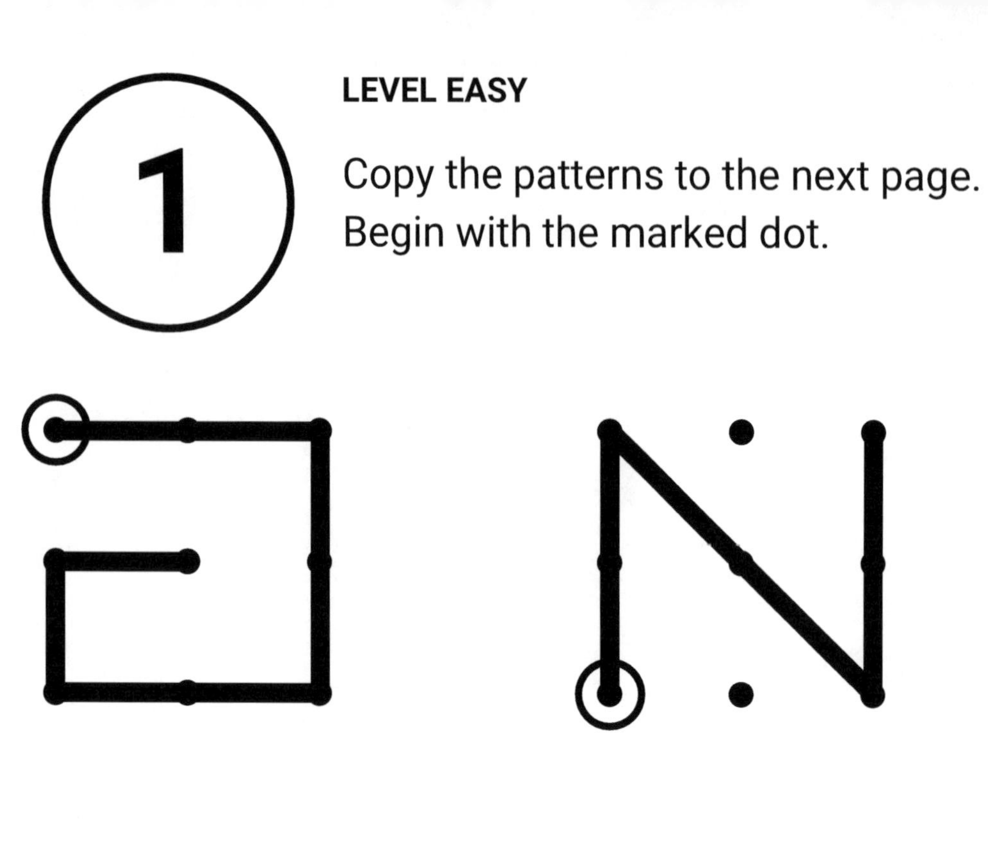

LEVEL EASY

Copy the patterns to the next page.
Begin with the marked dot.

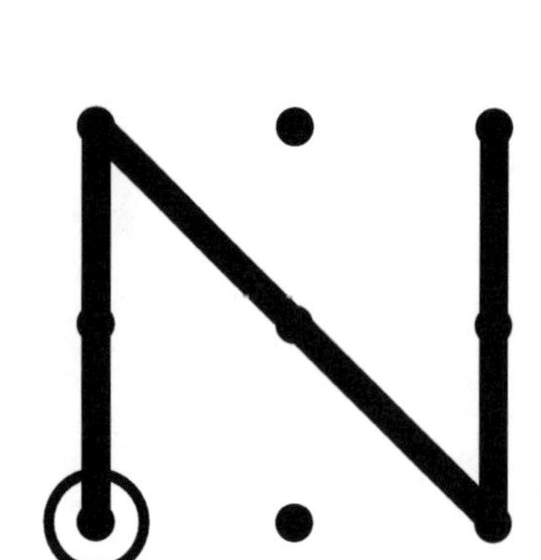

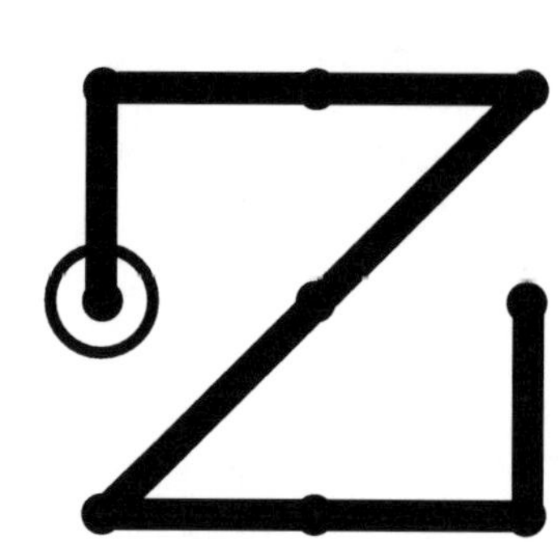

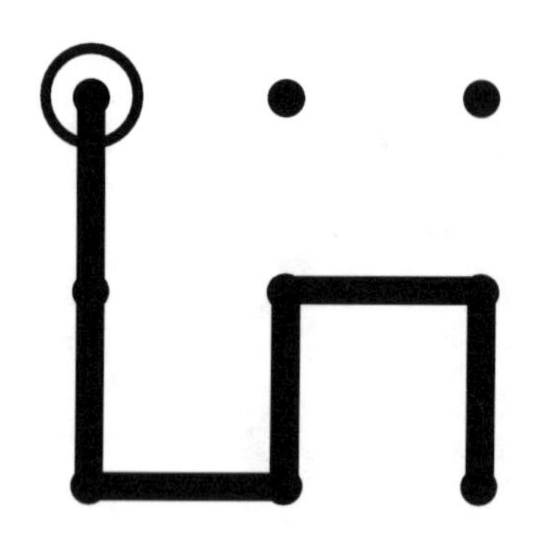

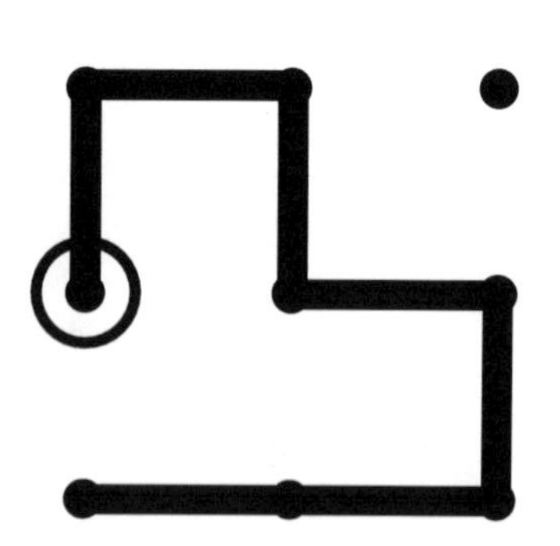

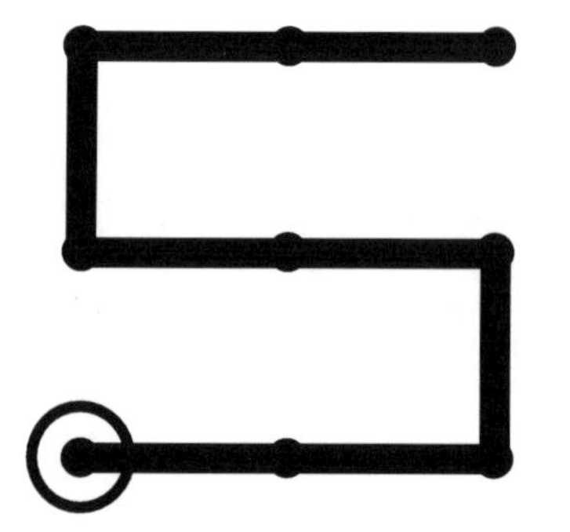

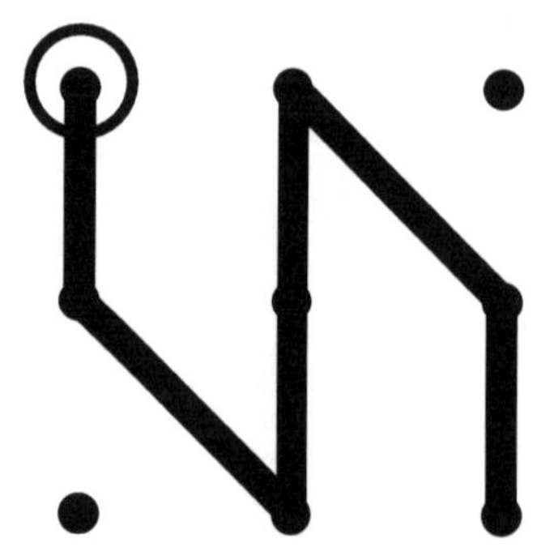

1

LEVEL EASY

LEVEL EASY

Copy the patterns to the next page.
Begin with the marked dot.

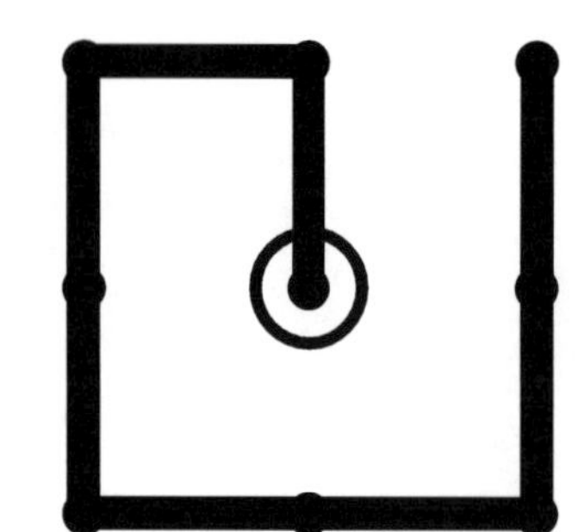
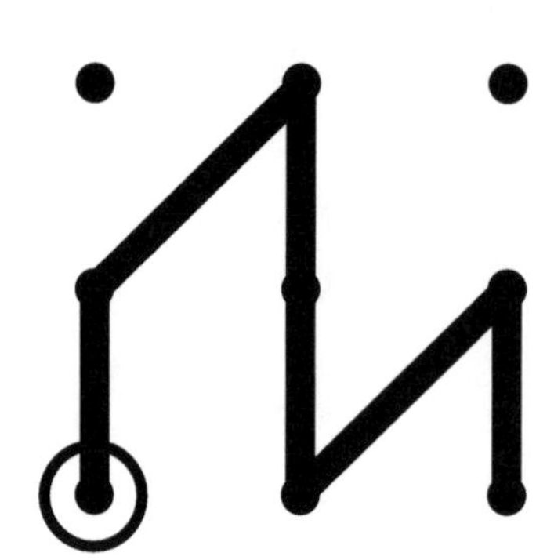

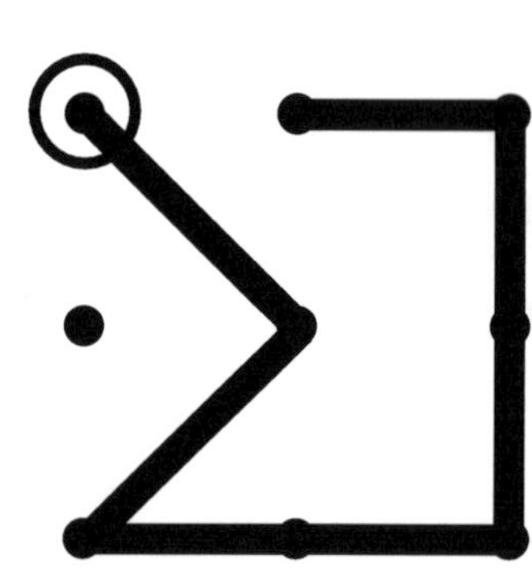

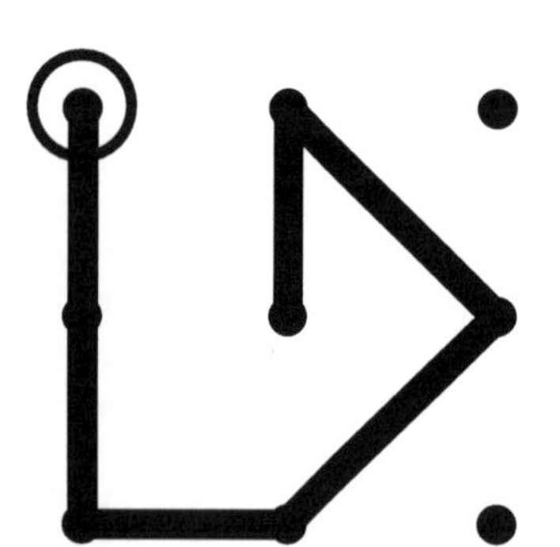

2

LEVEL EASY

LEVEL EASY

Copy the patterns to the next page.
Begin with the marked dot.

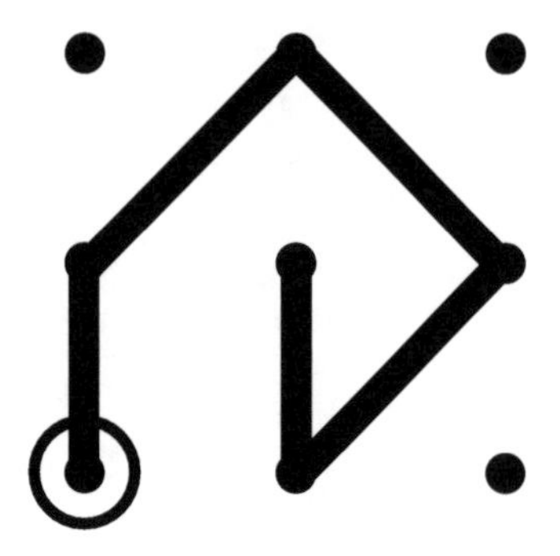

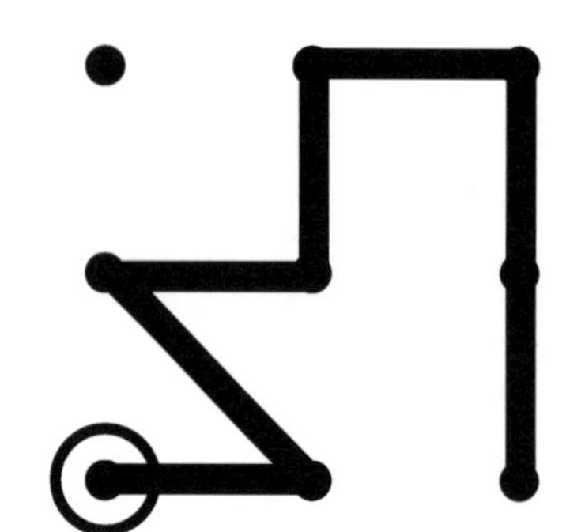

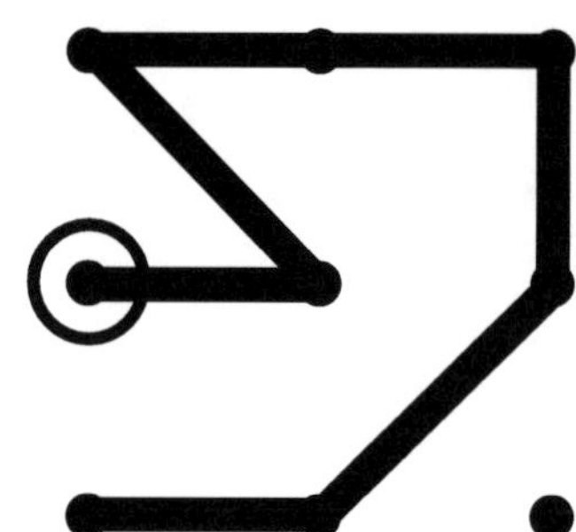

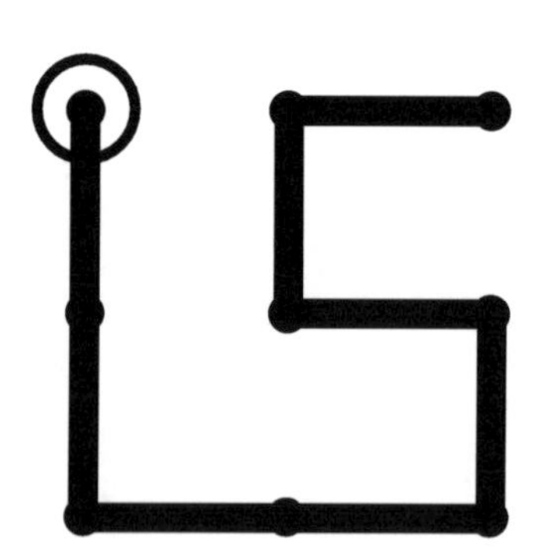

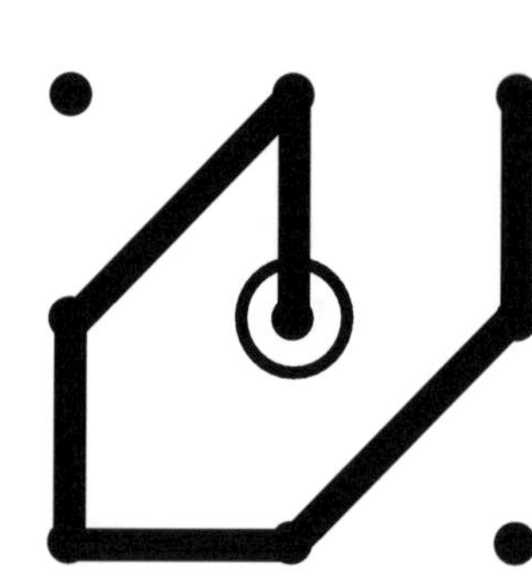

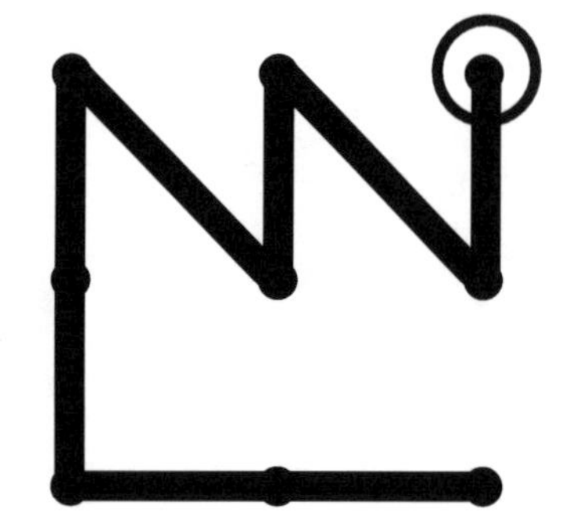

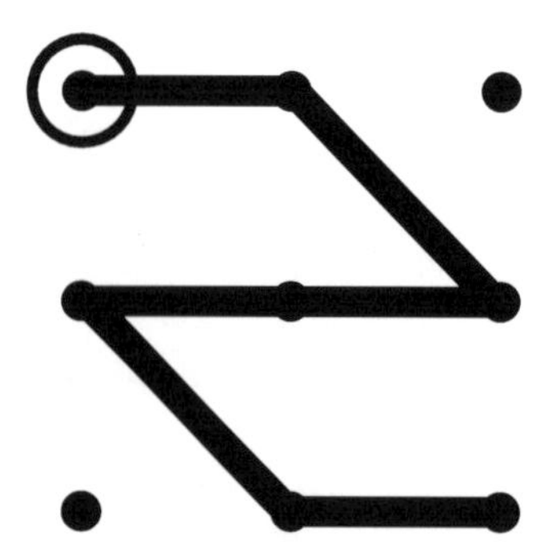

3

LEVEL EASY

LEVEL EASY

Copy the patterns to the next page.
Begin with the marked dot.

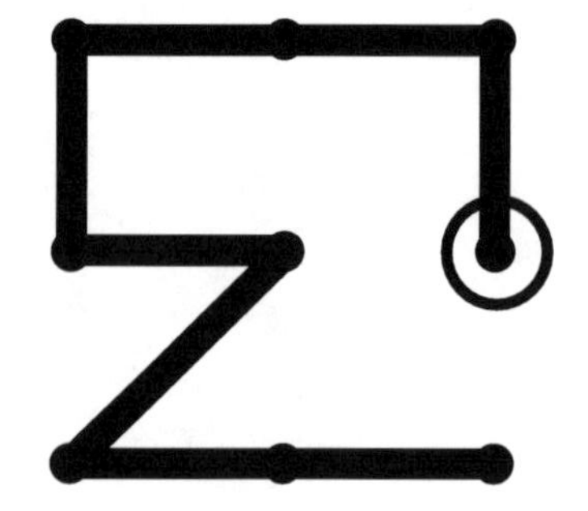

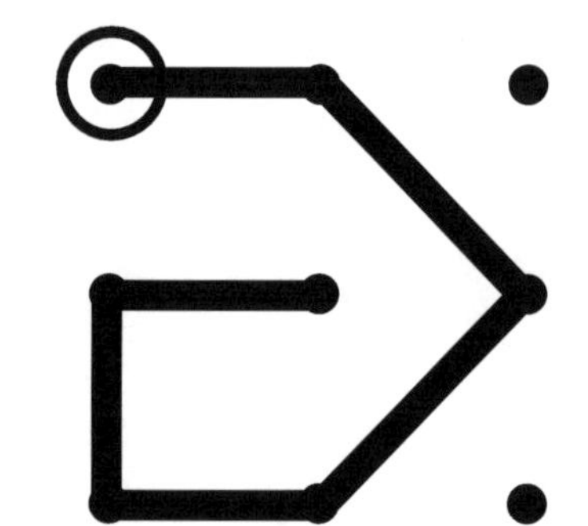

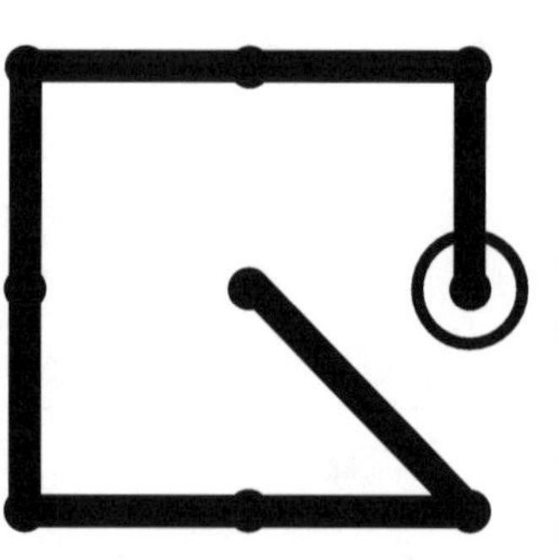

4

LEVEL EASY

LEVEL EASY

Copy the patterns to the next page.
Begin with the marked dot.

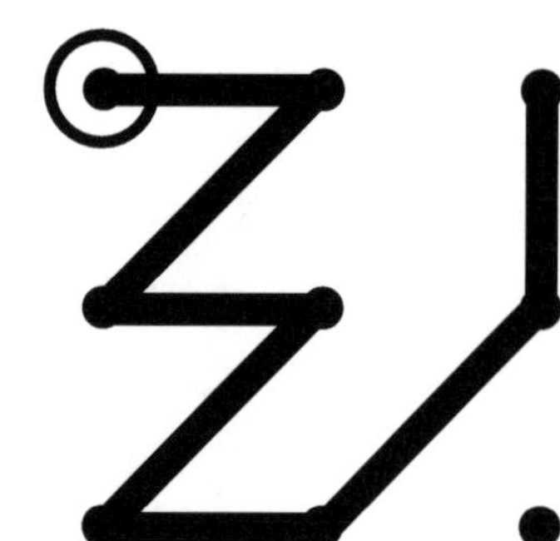

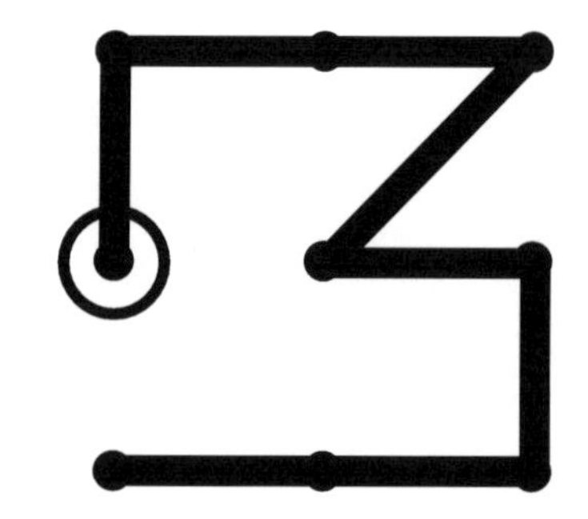

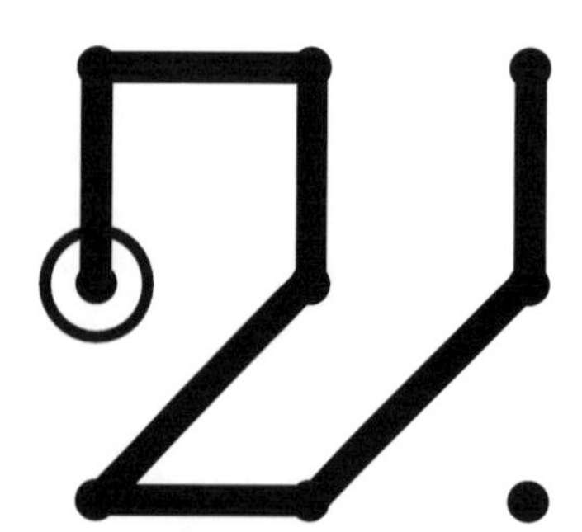

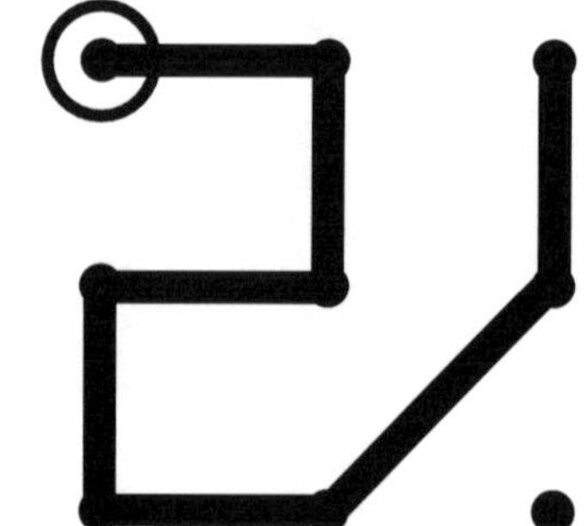

5

LEVEL EASY

6

LEVEL EASY

Copy the patterns to the next page.
Begin with the marked dot.

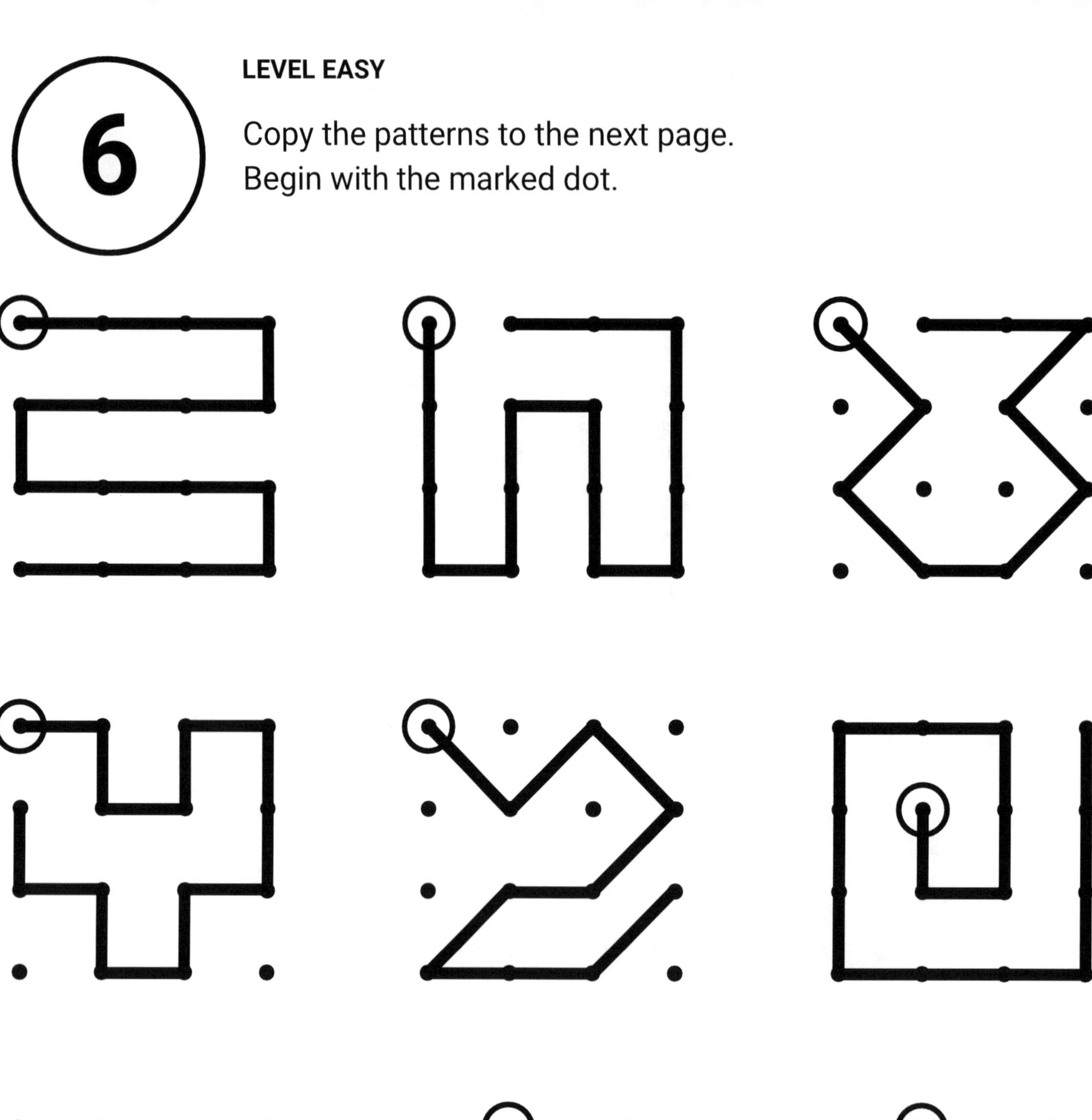

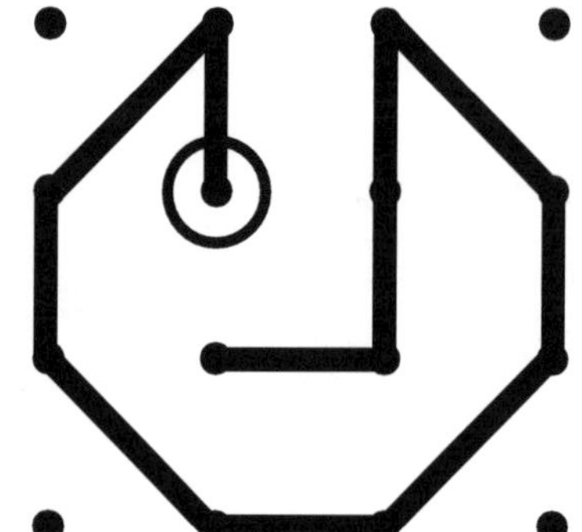

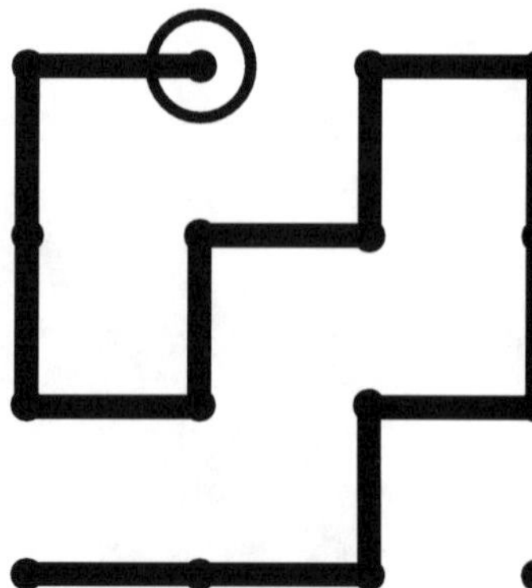

LEVEL EASY

TRACK AND COPY

Visual Treasure Chest

LEVEL EASY

Copy the patterns to the next page.
Begin with the marked dot.

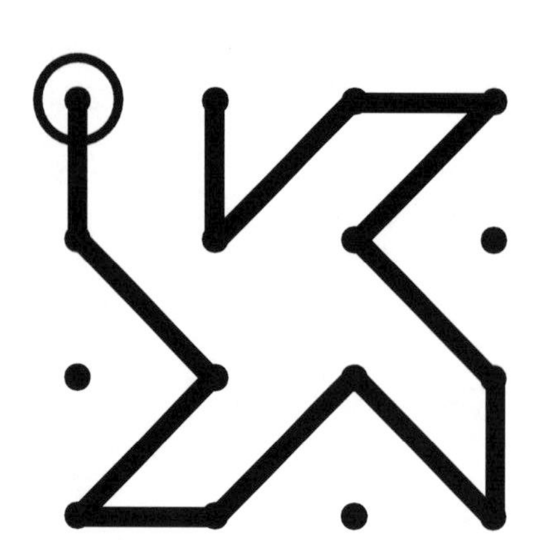
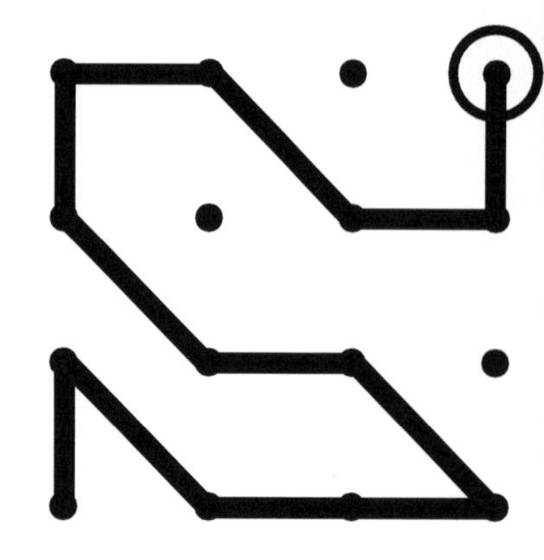
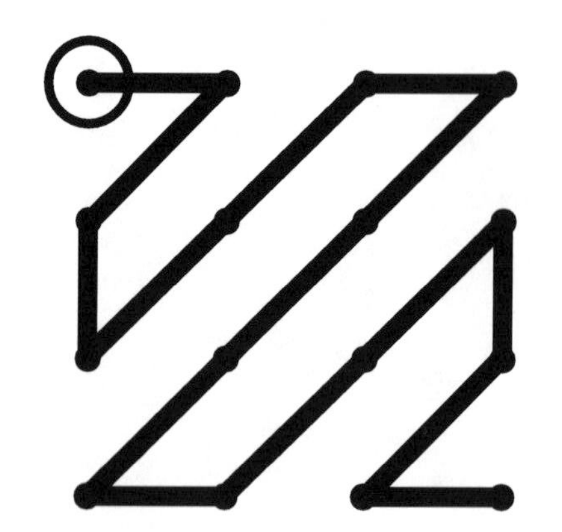
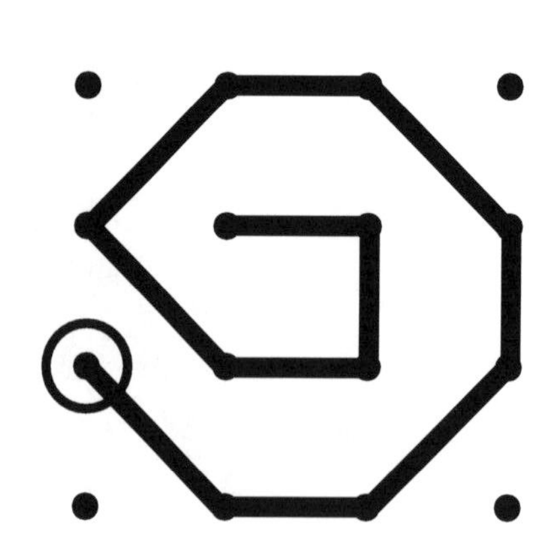
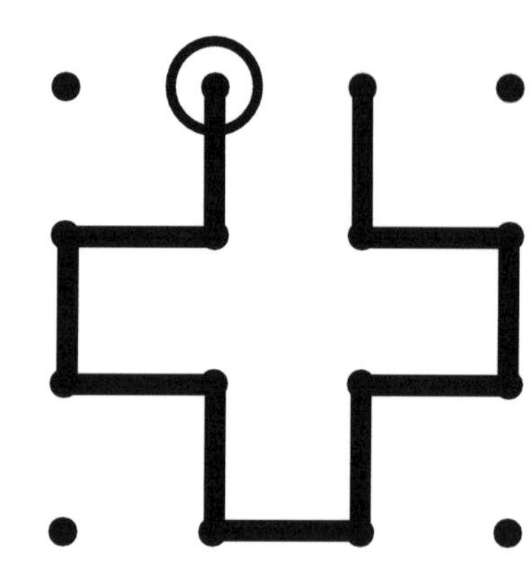

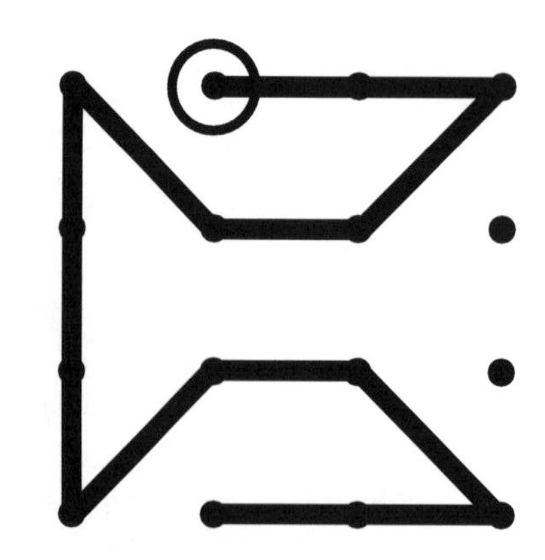
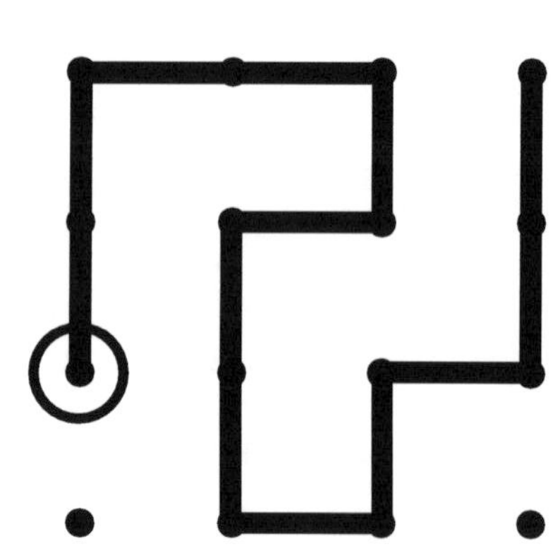

LEVEL EASY

TRACK AND COPY

Visual Treasure Chest

LEVEL EASY

Copy the patterns to the next page.
Begin with the marked dot.

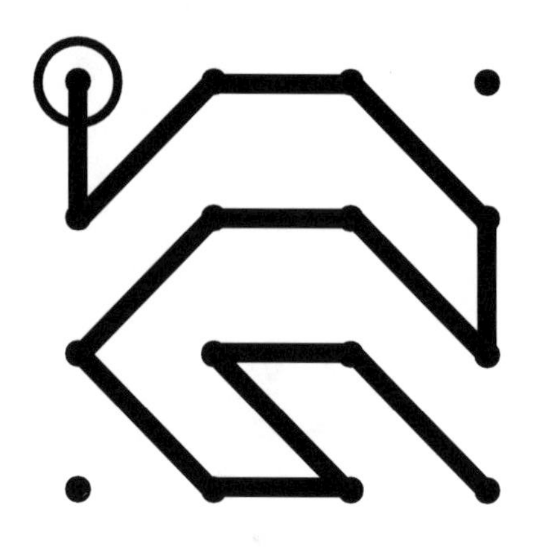
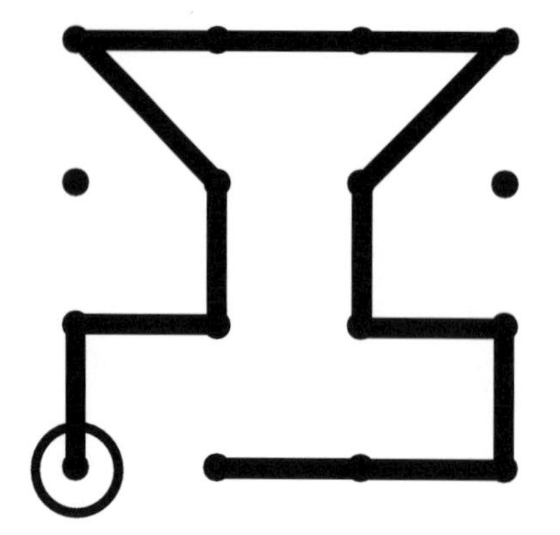
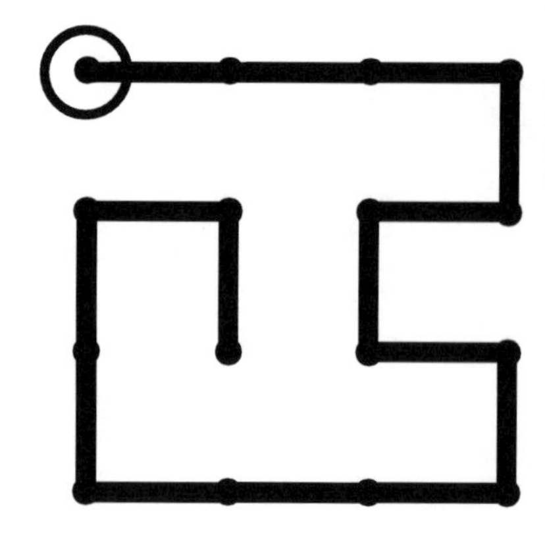

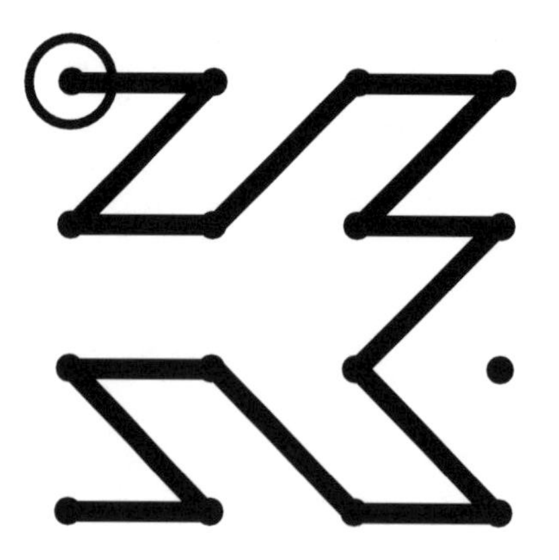
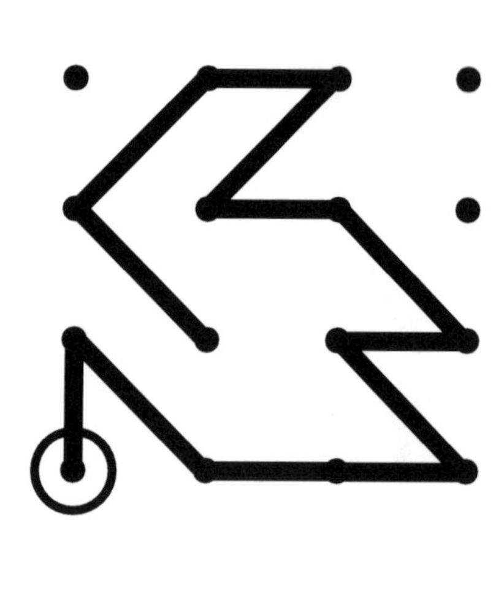

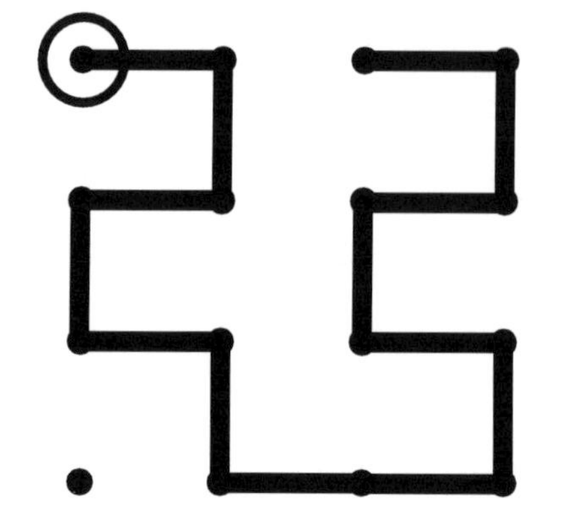
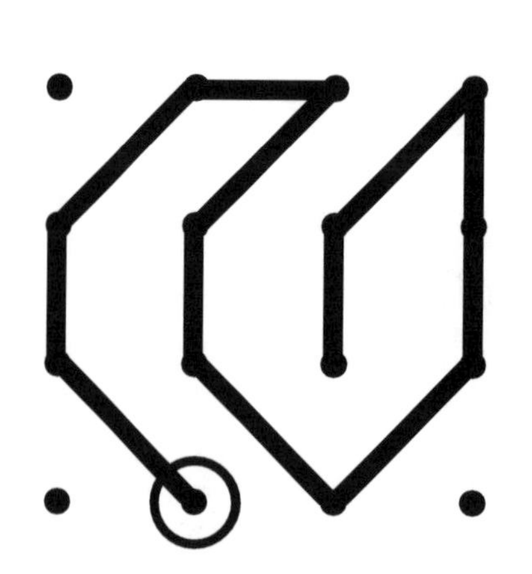

8

LEVEL EASY

TRACK AND COPY

Visual Treasure Chest

LEVEL EASY

Copy the patterns to the next page.
Begin with the marked dot.

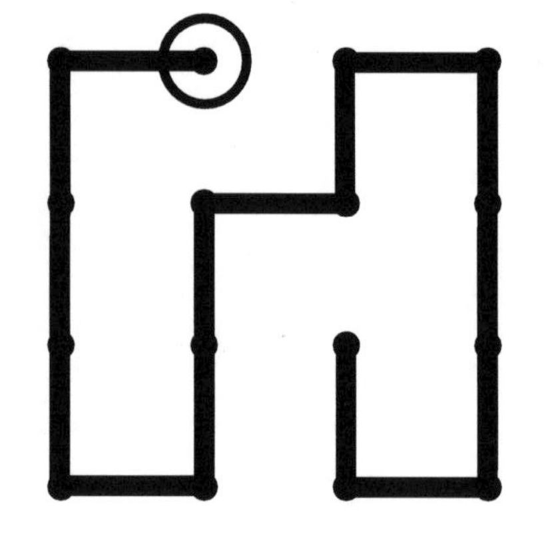
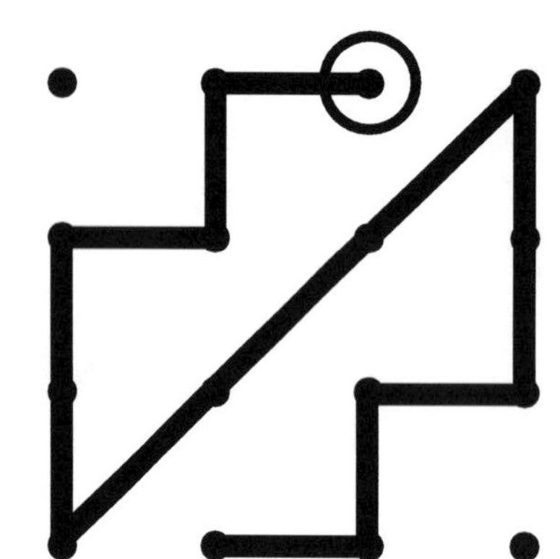
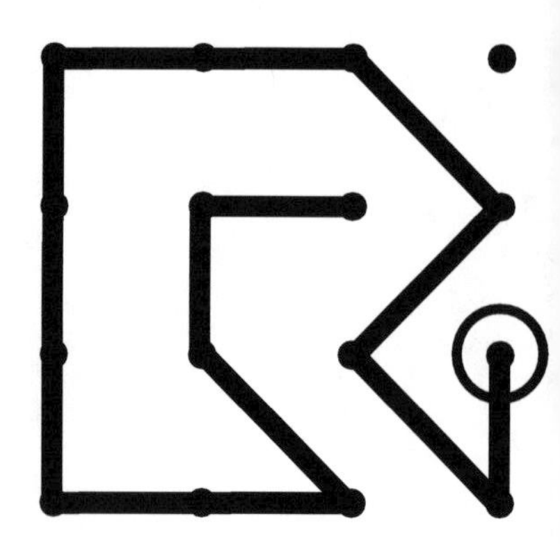

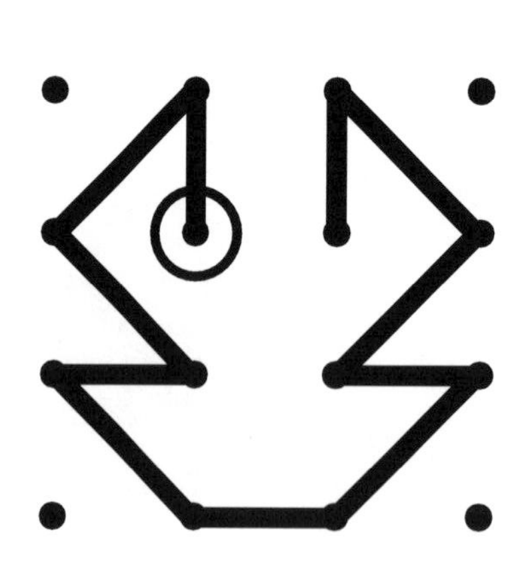
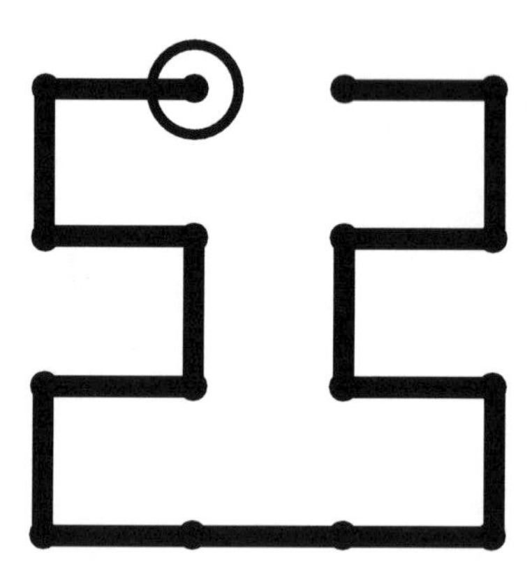

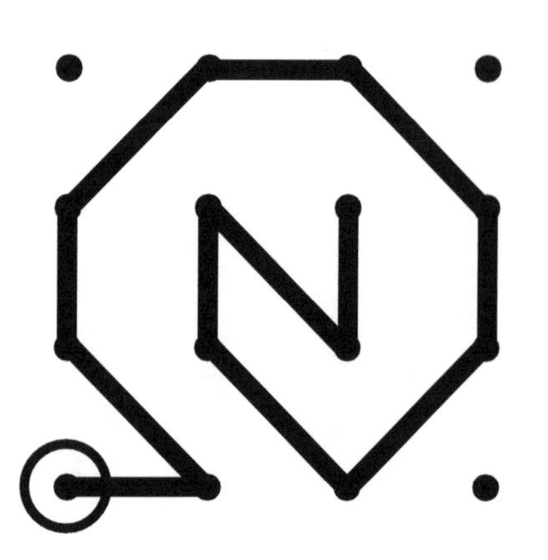
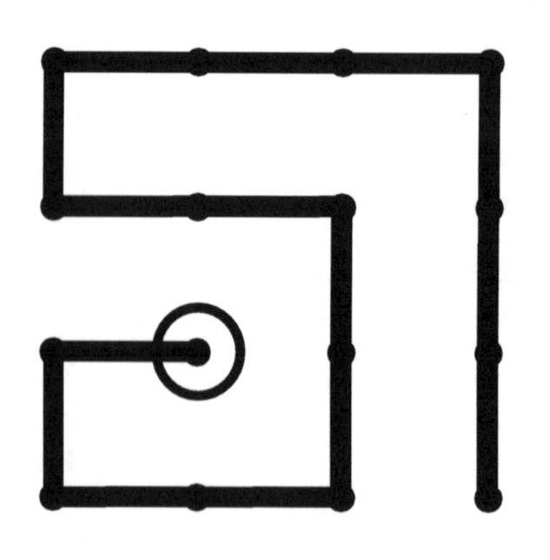

9

LEVEL EASY

TRACK AND COPY

Visual Treasure Chest

LEVEL EASY

Copy the patterns to the next page.
Begin with the marked dot.

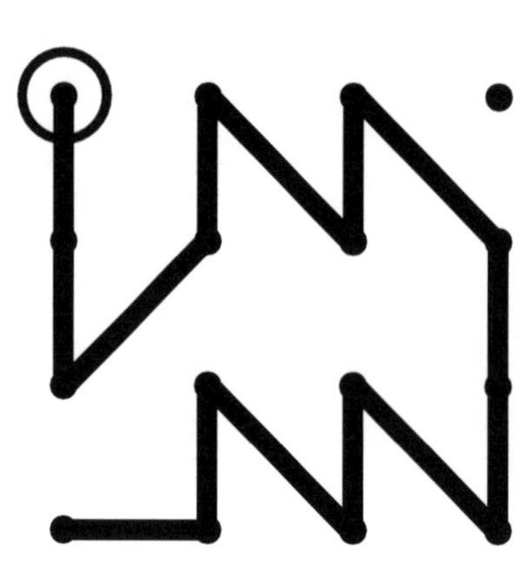

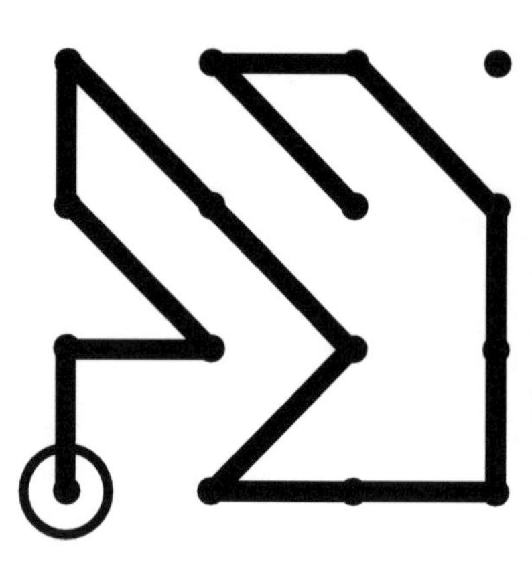

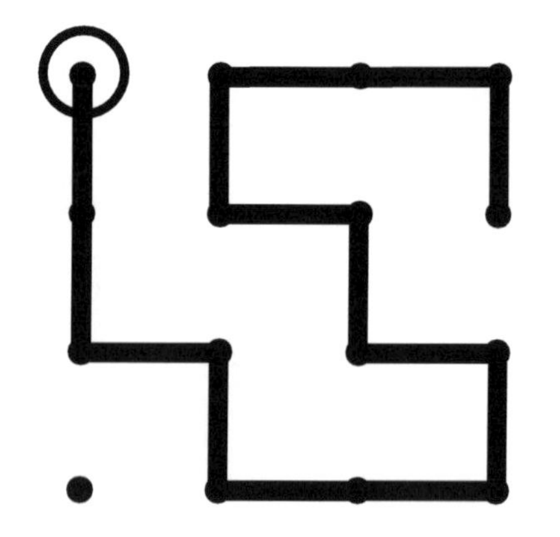

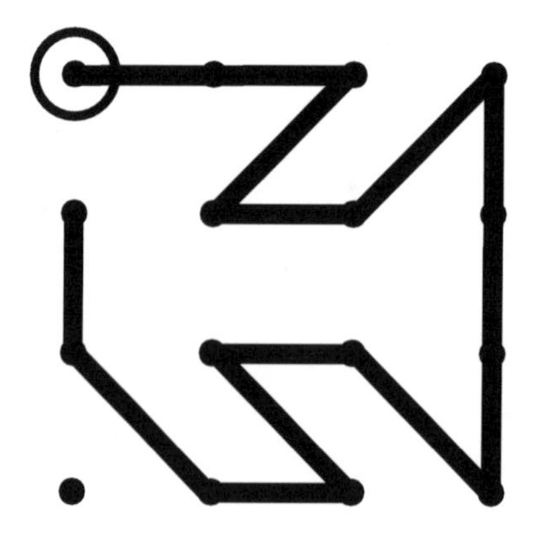

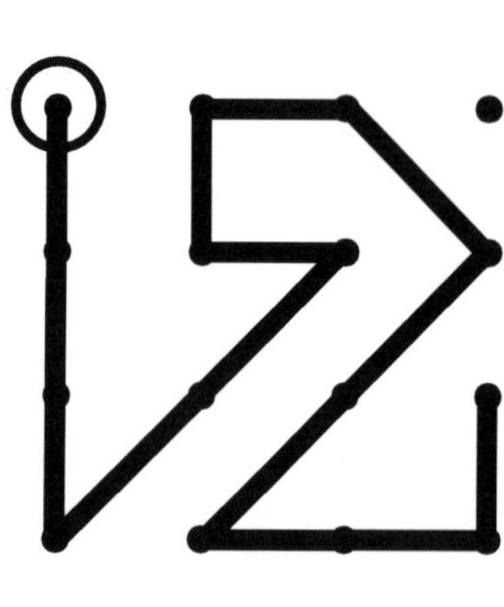

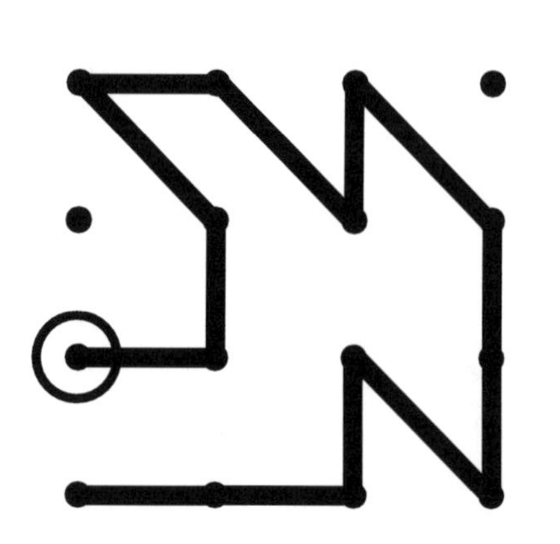

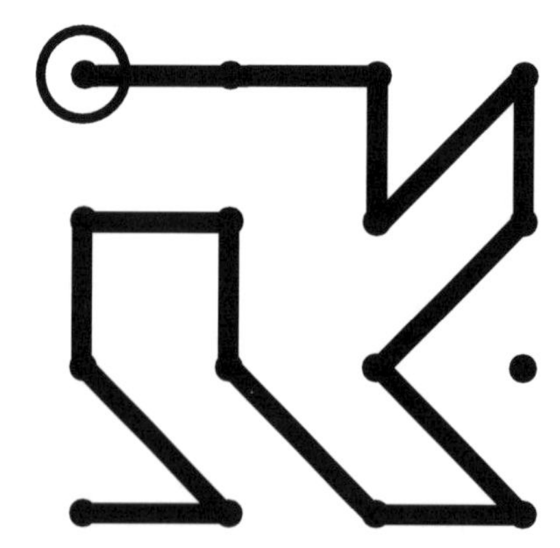

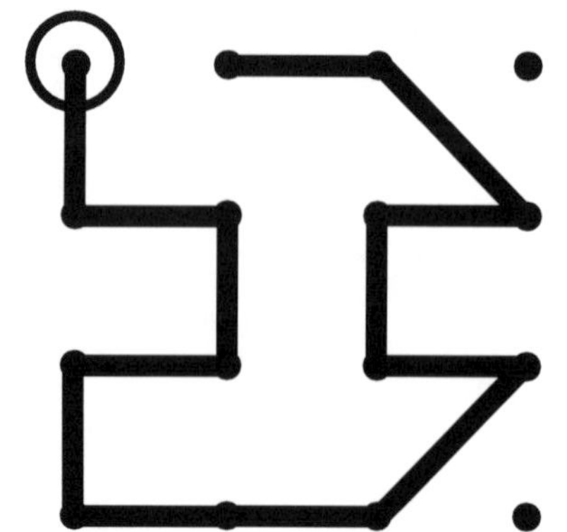

LEVEL EASY

TRACK AND COPY

11

LEVEL MEDIUM

Copy each pattern to the grid beside it.
Begin with the marked dot.

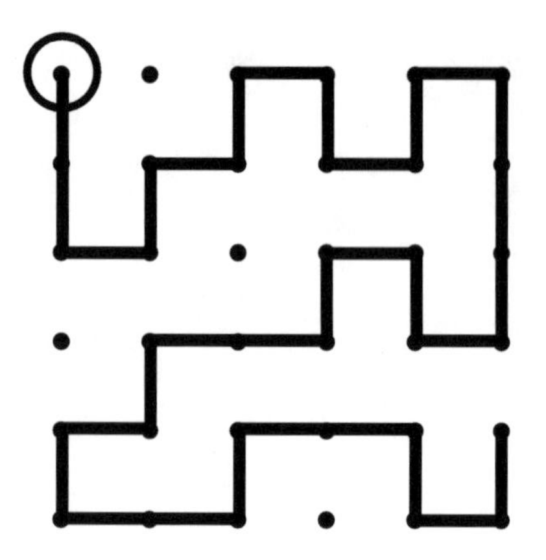

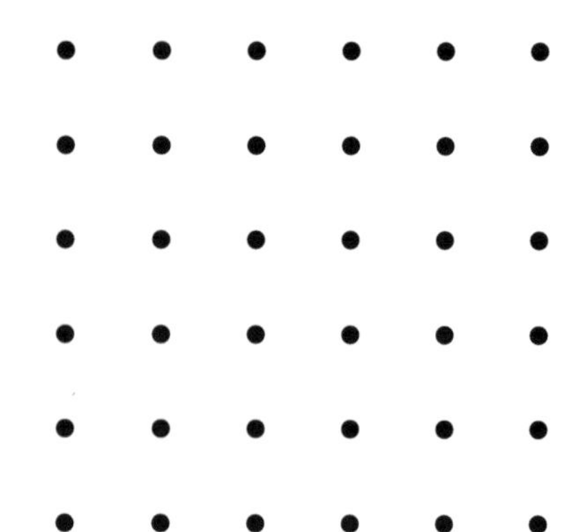

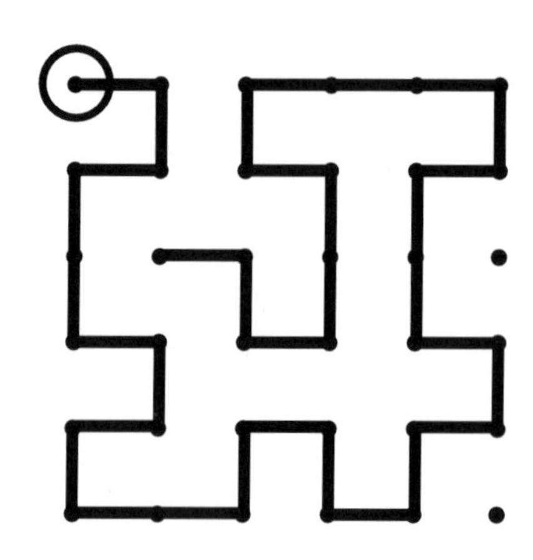

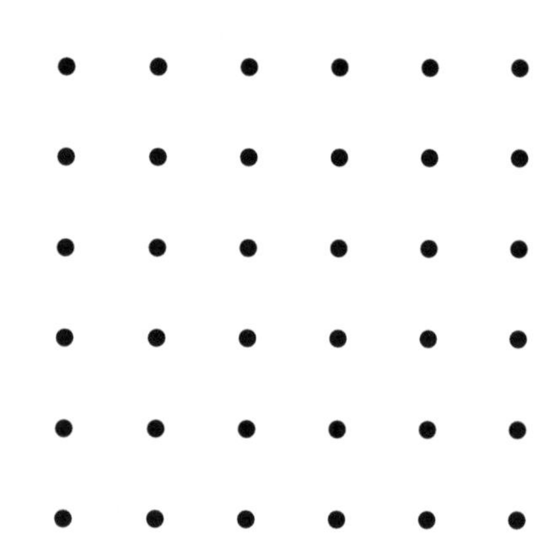

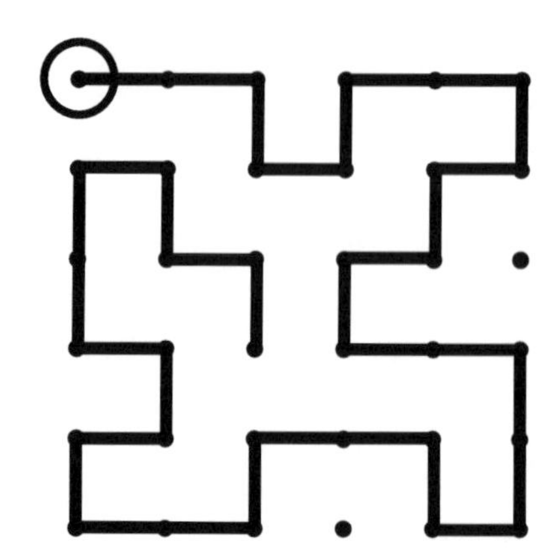

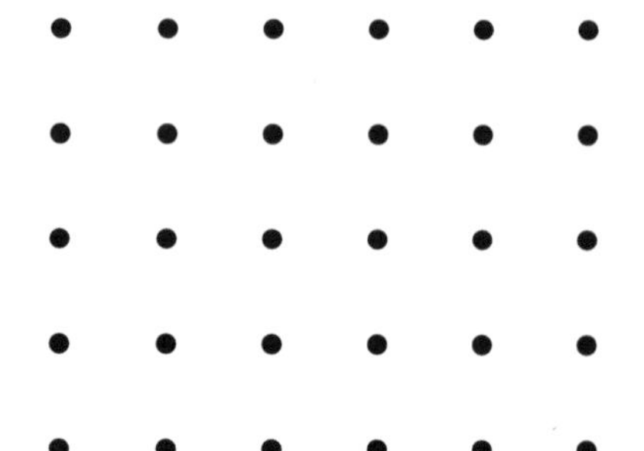

12

LEVEL MEDIUM

Copy each pattern to the grid beside it.
Begin with the marked dot.

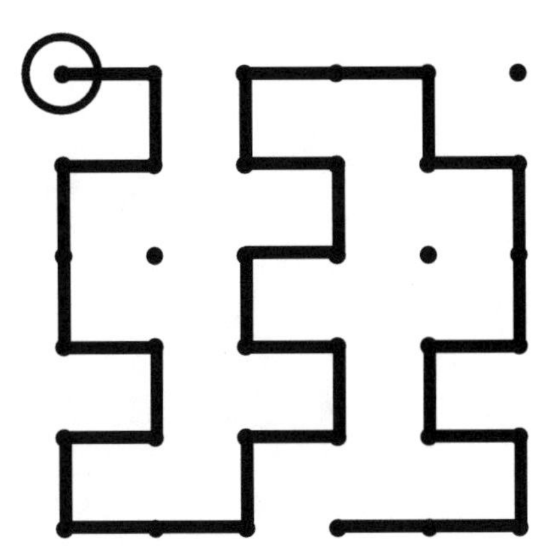

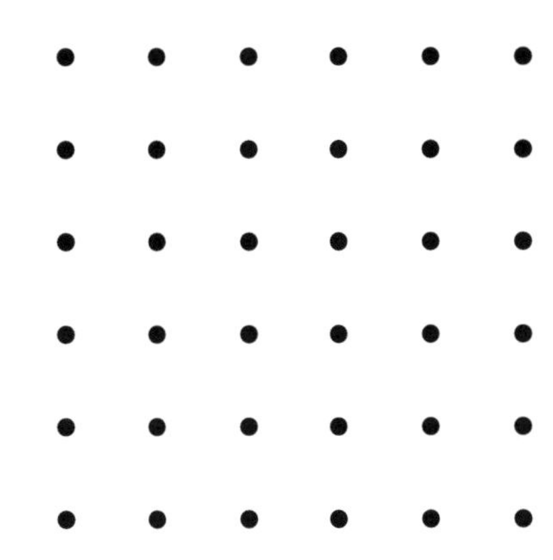

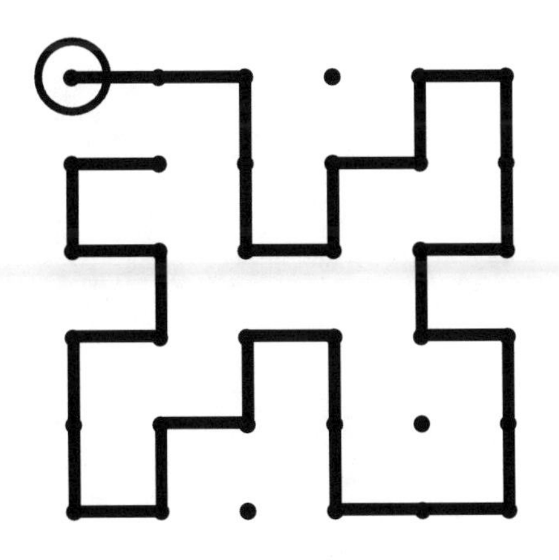

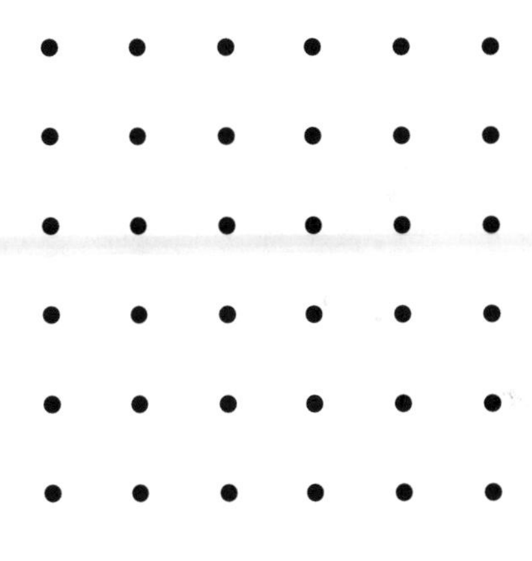

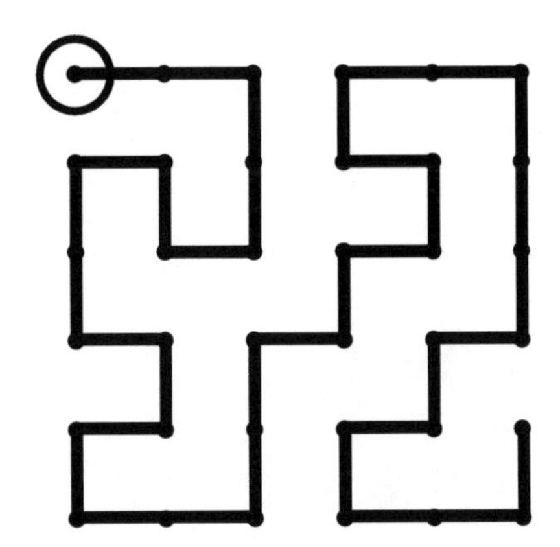

13

LEVEL MEDIUM

Copy each pattern to the grid beside it.
Begin with the marked dot.

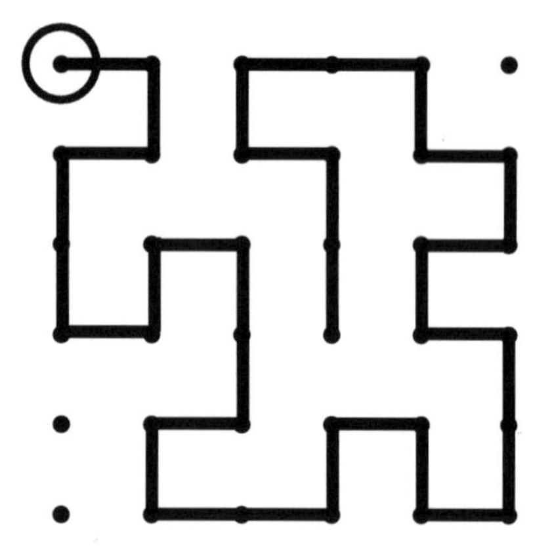

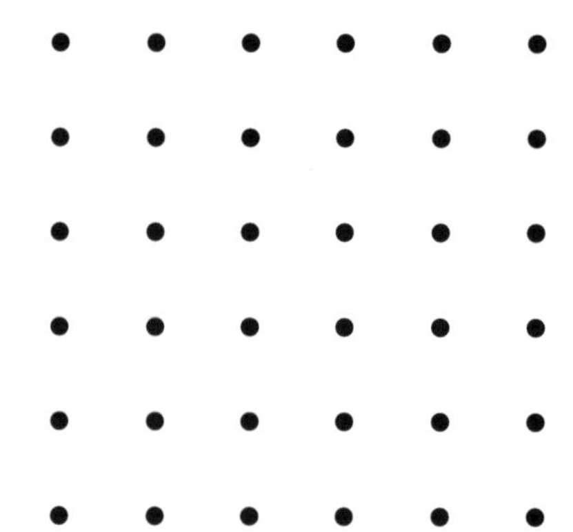

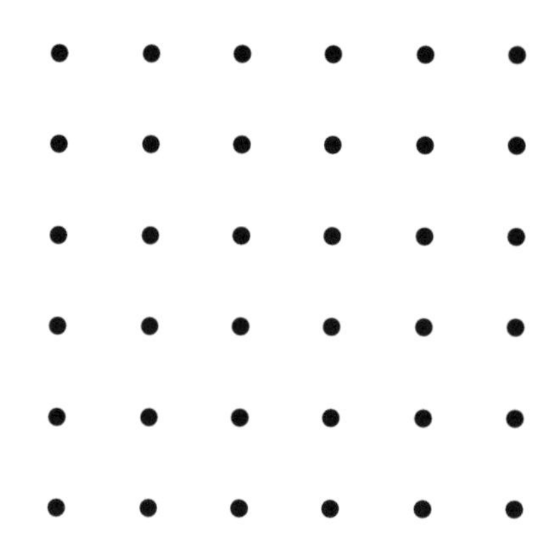

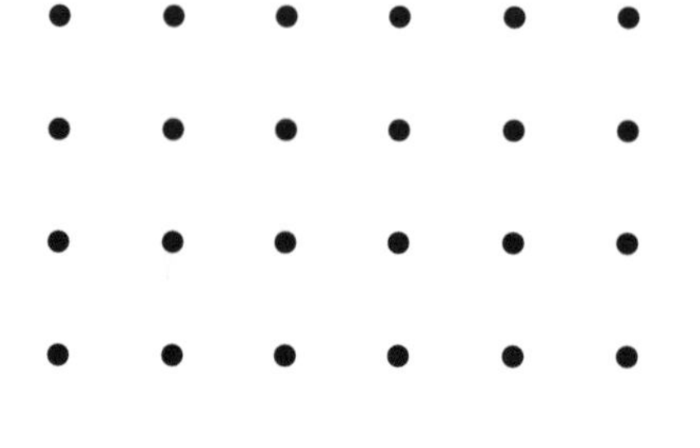

14

LEVEL MEDIUM

Copy each pattern to the grid beside it.
Begin with the marked dot.

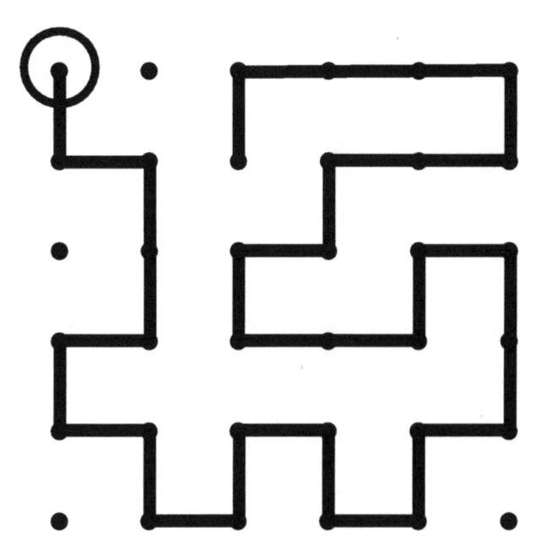

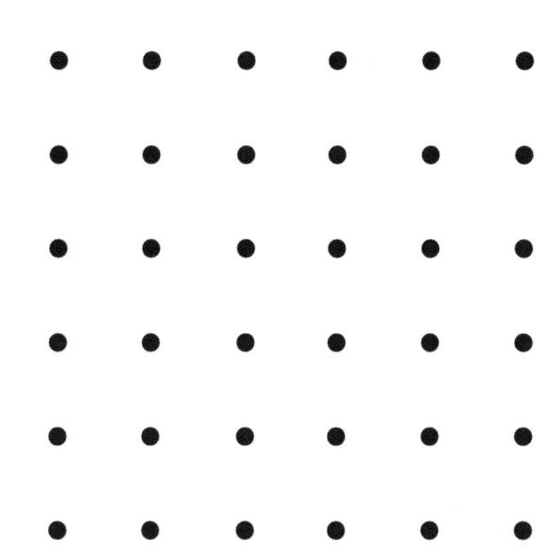

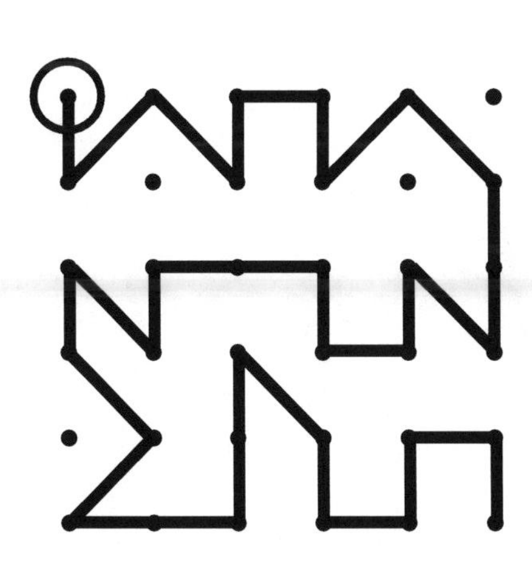

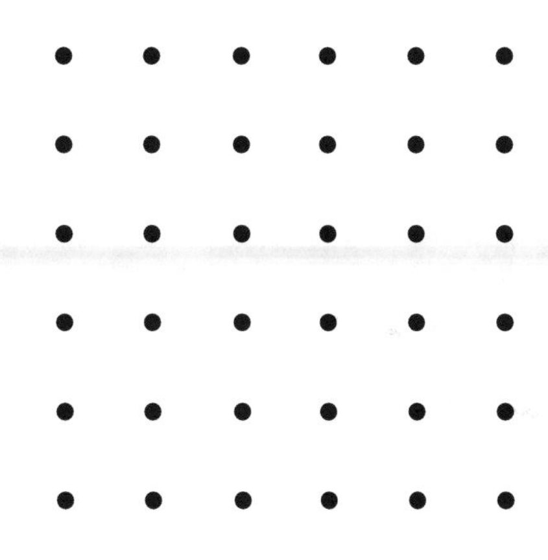

15

LEVEL MEDIUM

Copy each pattern to the grid beside it.
Begin with the marked dot.

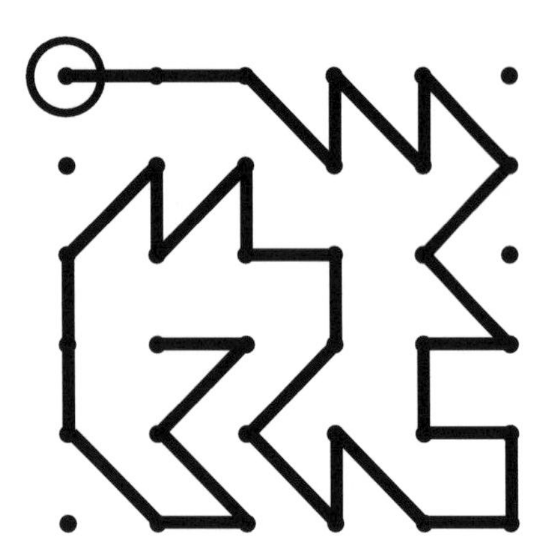

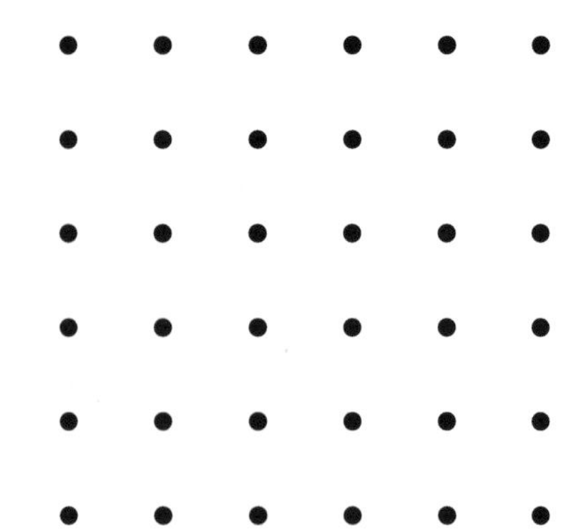

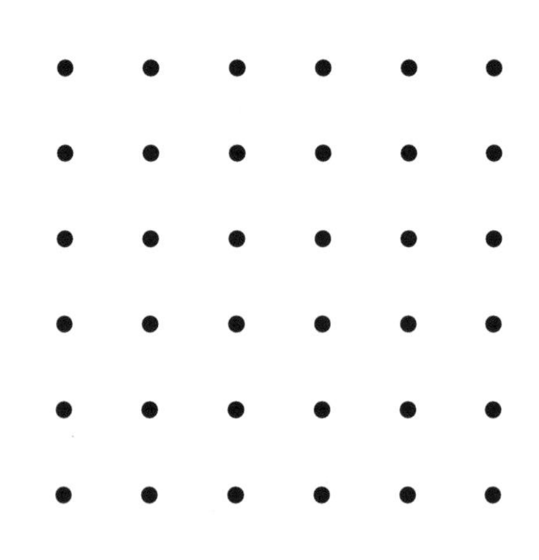

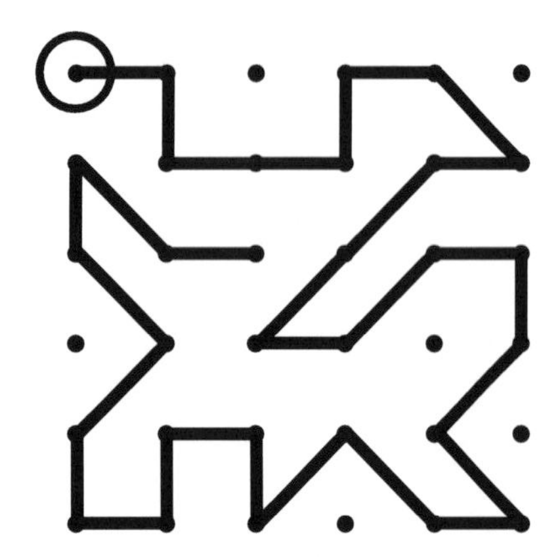

16

LEVEL MEDIUM

Copy each pattern to the grid beside it.
Begin with the marked dot.

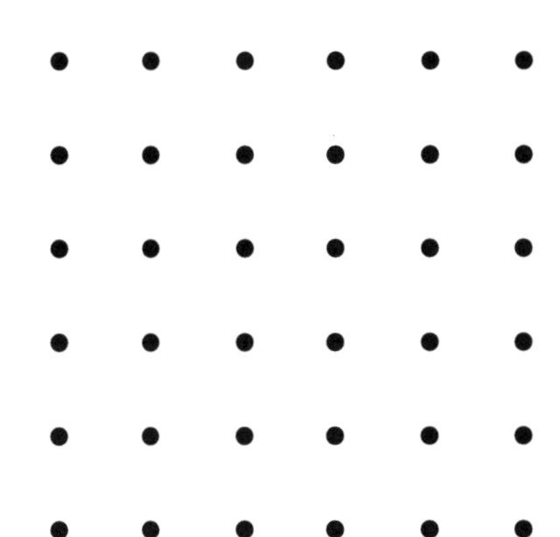

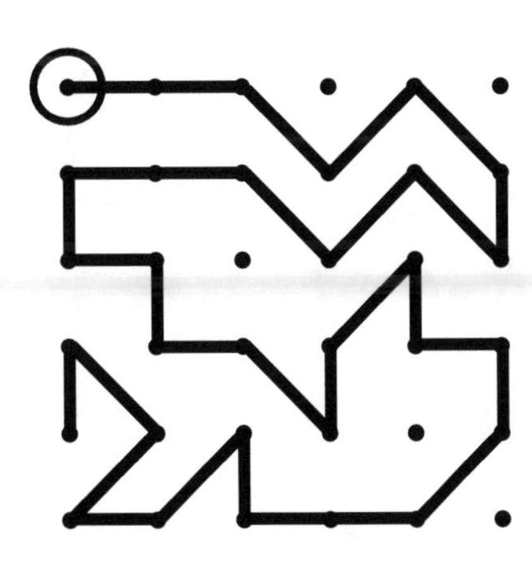

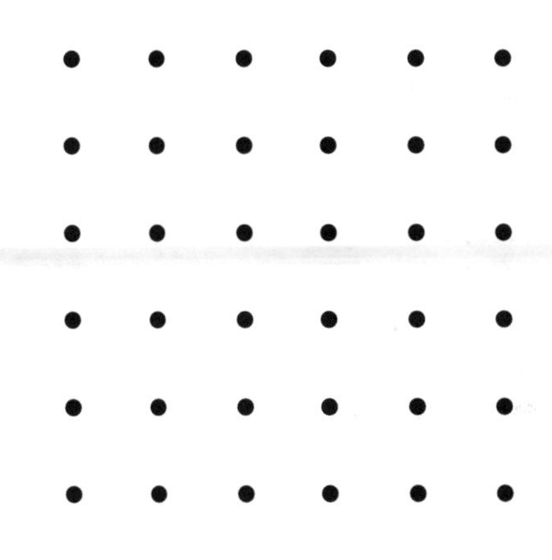

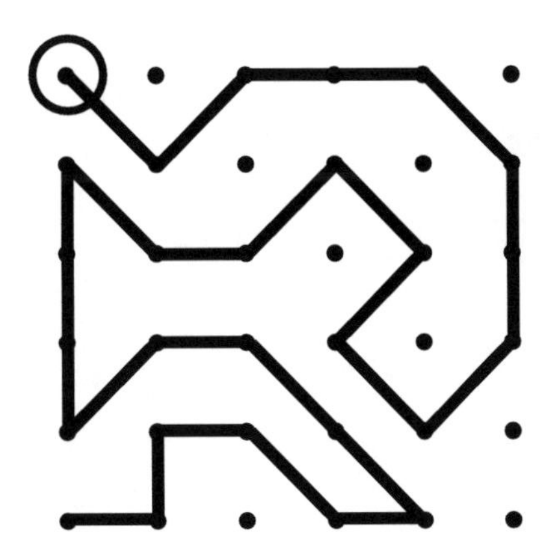

17

LEVEL MEDIUM

Copy each pattern to the grid beside it.
Begin with the marked dot.

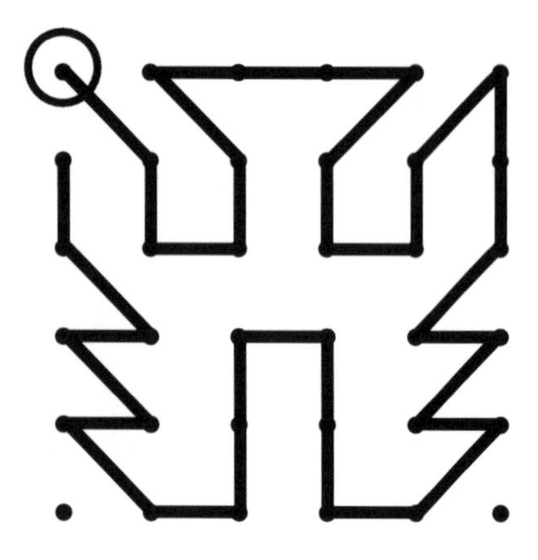

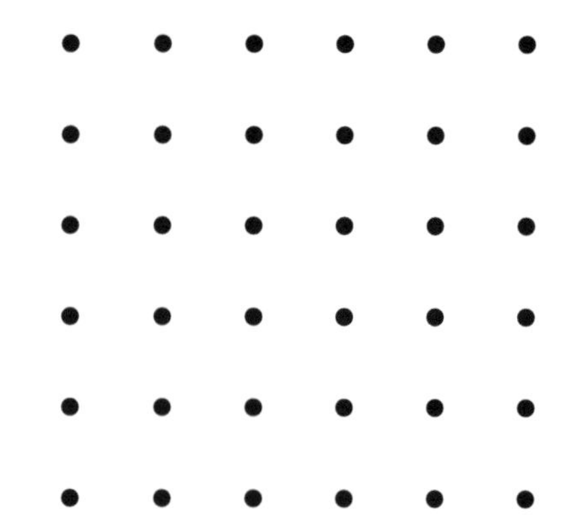

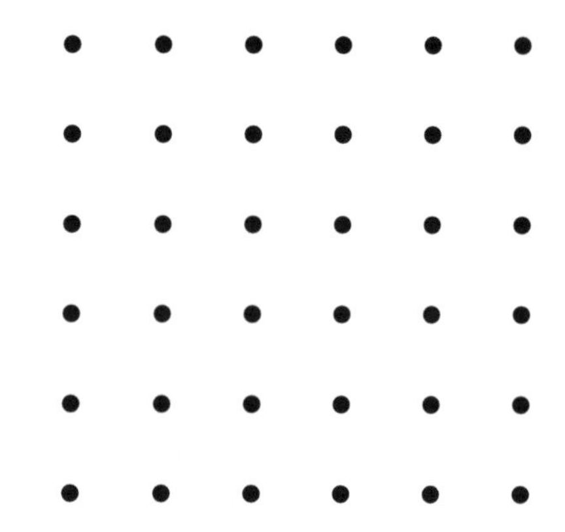

18

LEVEL MEDIUM

Copy each pattern to the grid beside it.
Begin with the marked dot.

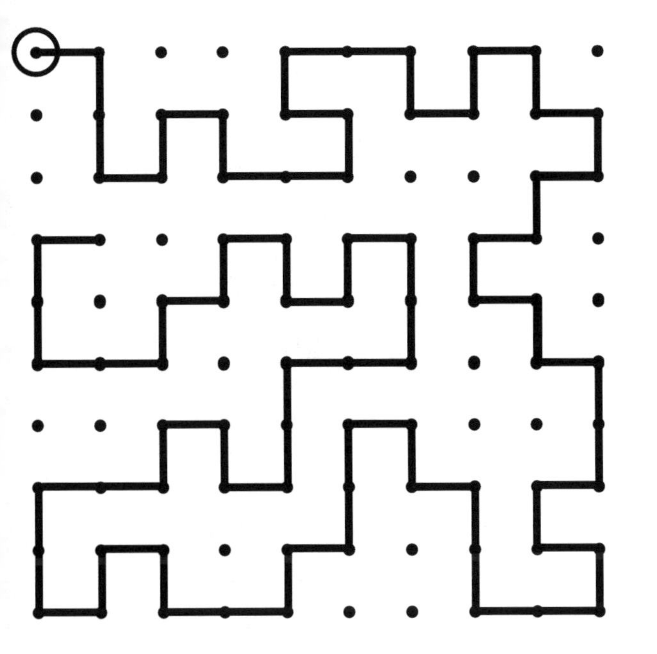

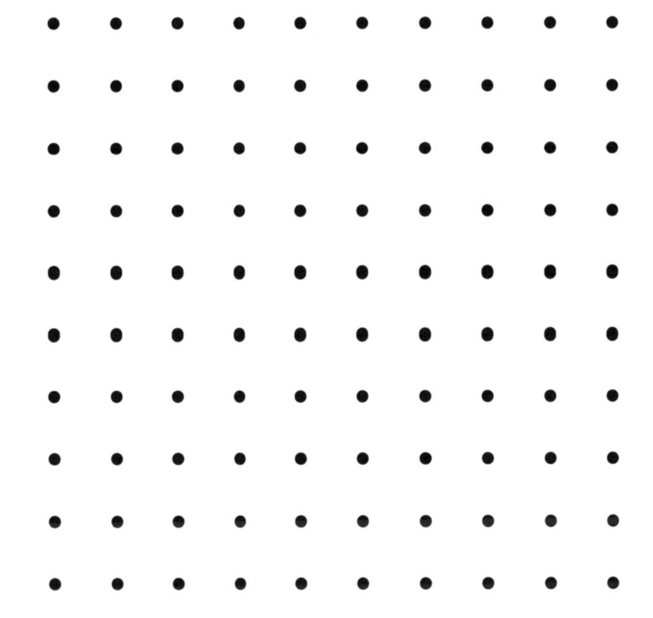

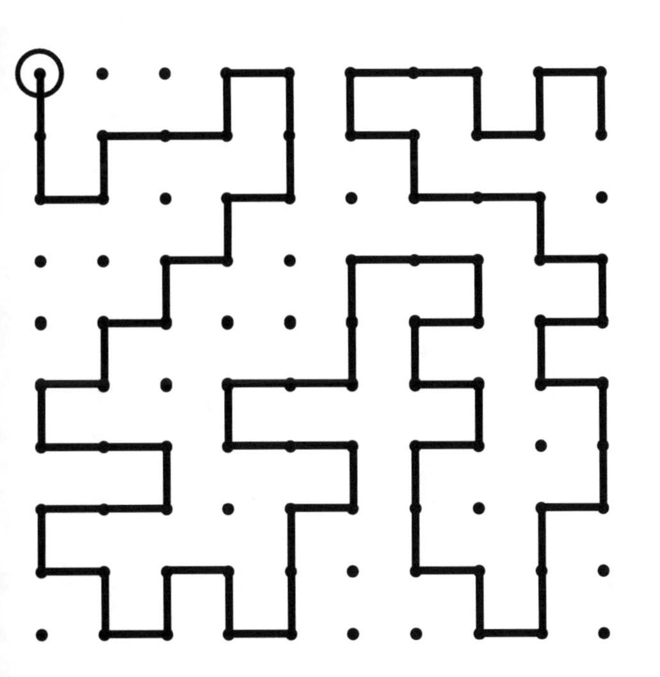

19

LEVEL MEDIUM

Copy each pattern to the grid beside it.
Begin with the marked dot.

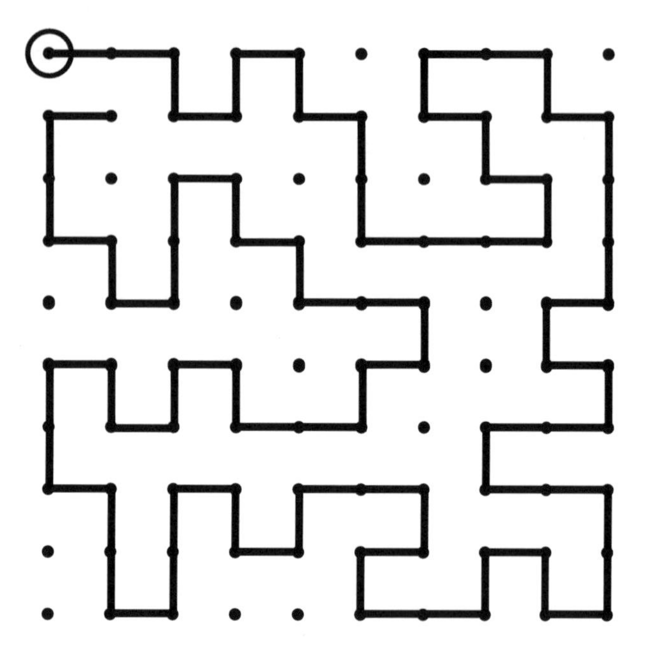
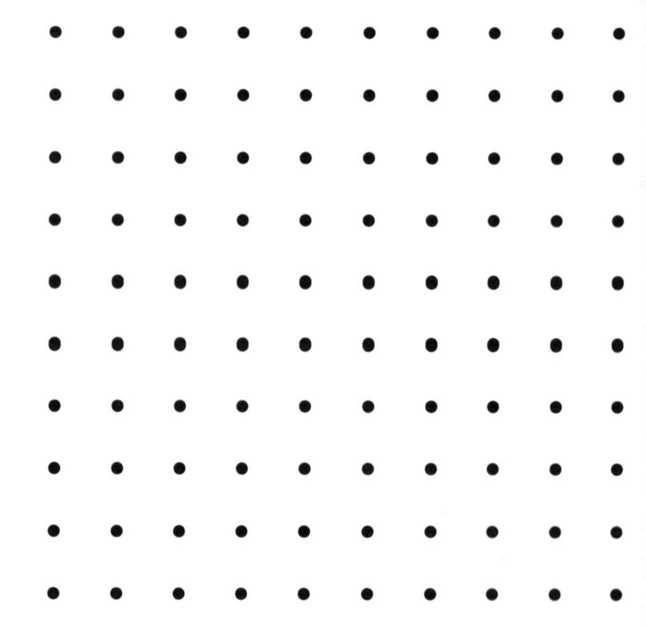

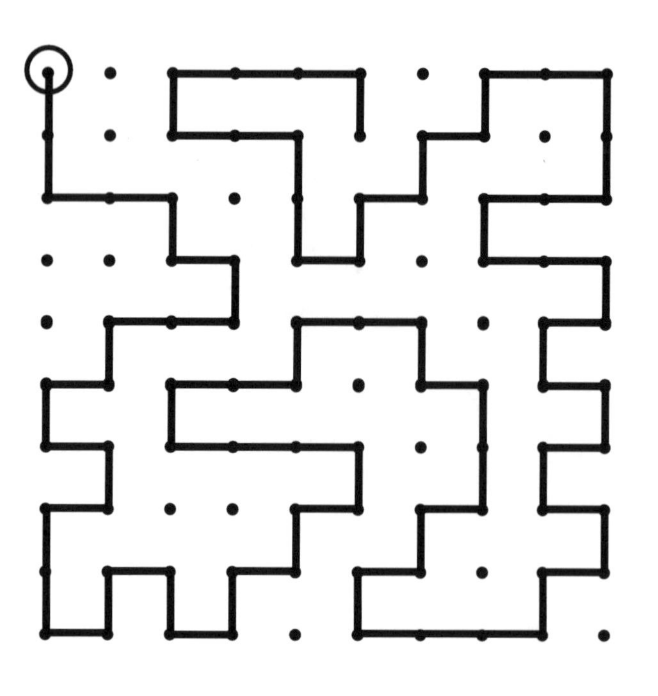

20

LEVEL MEDIUM

Copy each pattern to the grid beside it.
Begin with the marked dot.

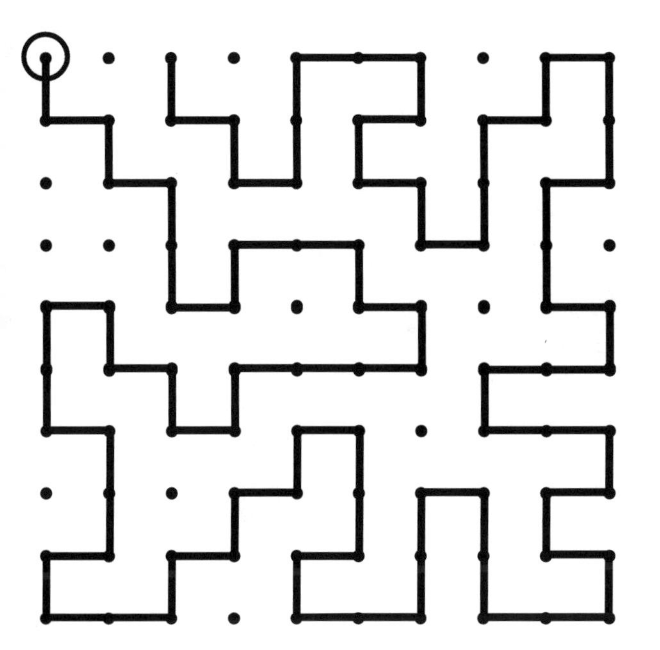

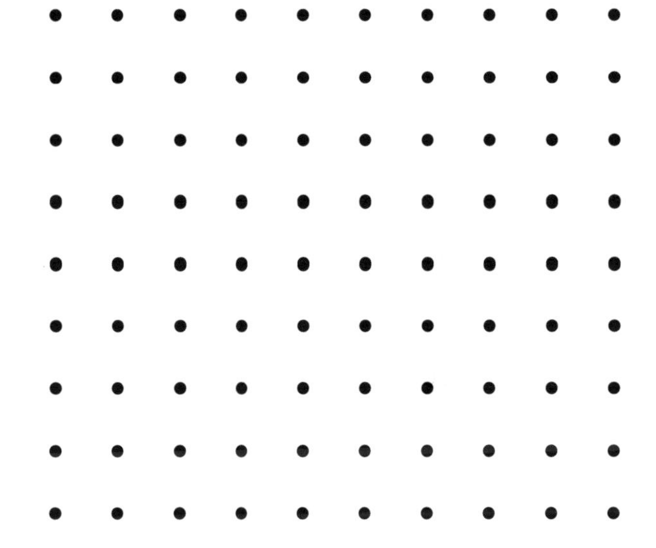

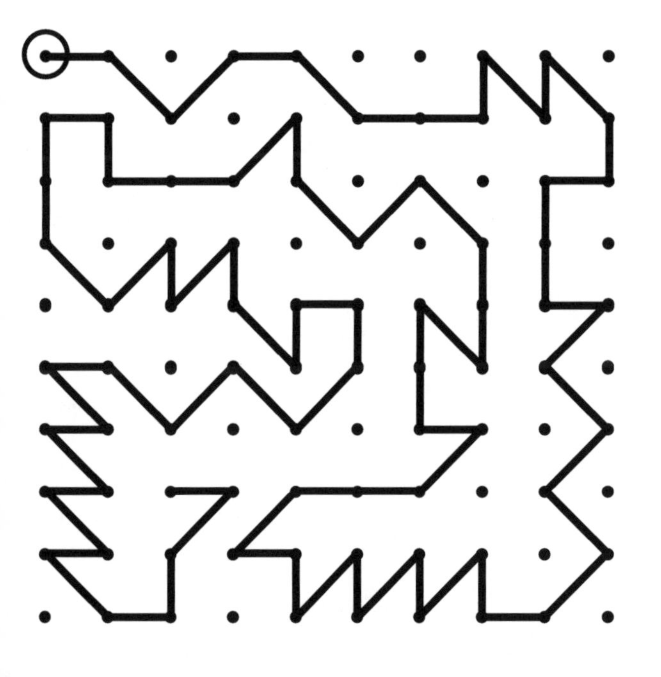

21

LEVEL MEDIUM

Copy each pattern to the grid beside it.
Begin with the marked dot.

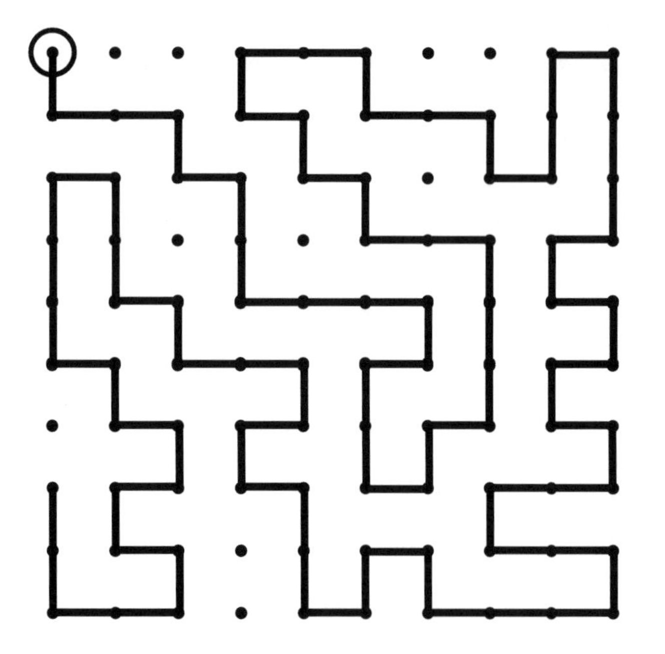

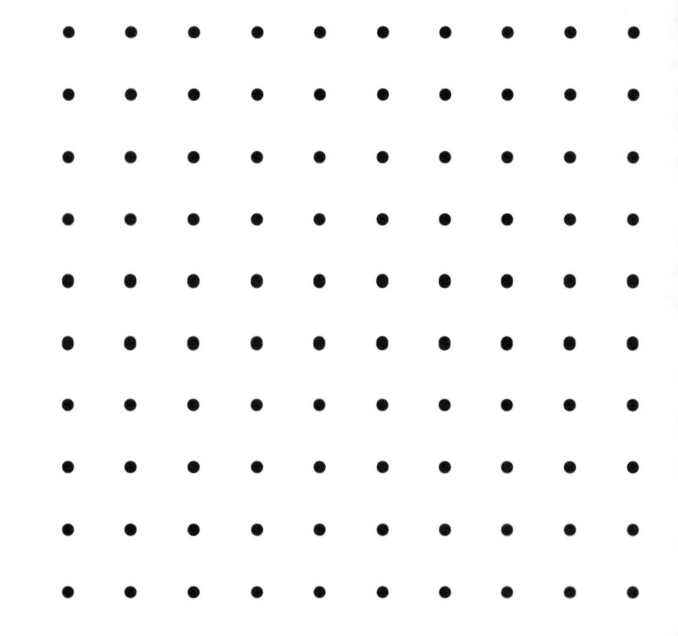

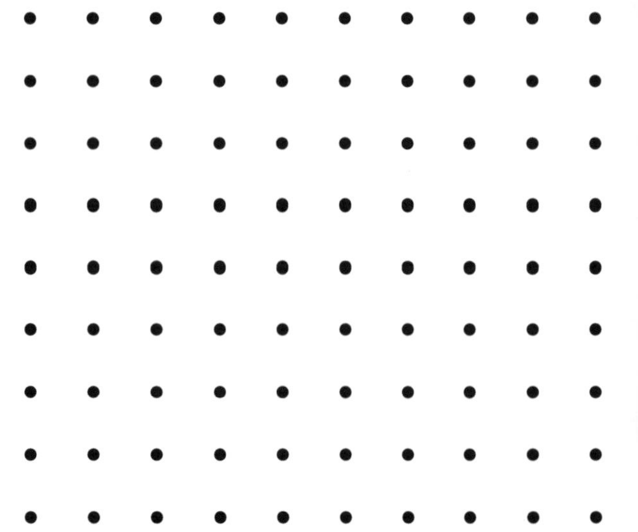

22

LEVEL MEDIUM

Copy each pattern to the grid beside it.
Begin with the marked dot.

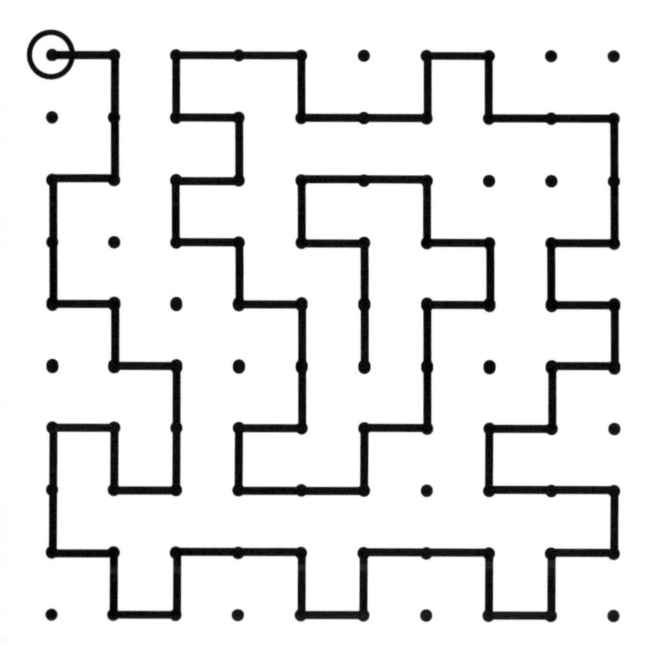

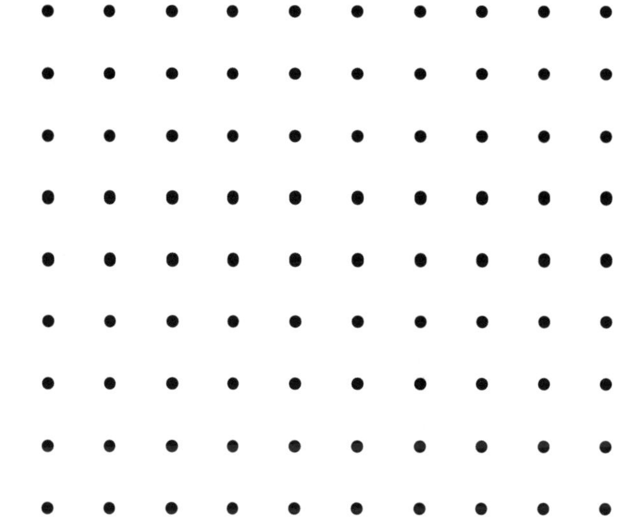

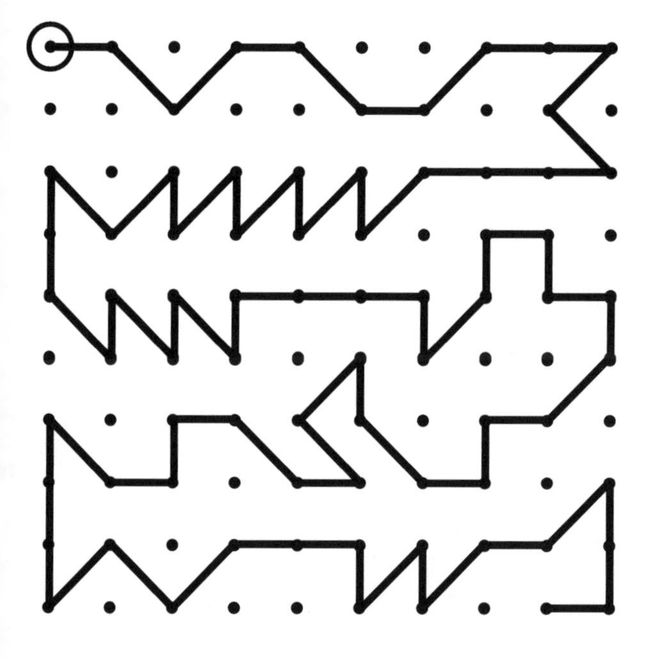

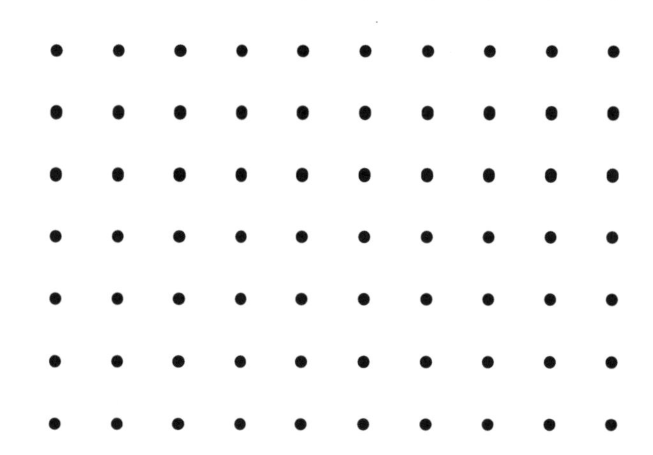

23

LEVEL MEDIUM

Copy each pattern to the grid beside it.
Begin with the marked dot.

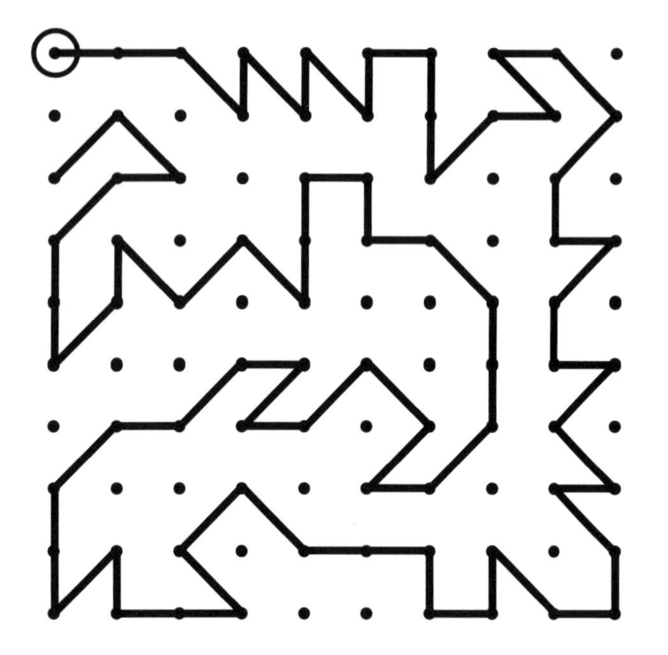

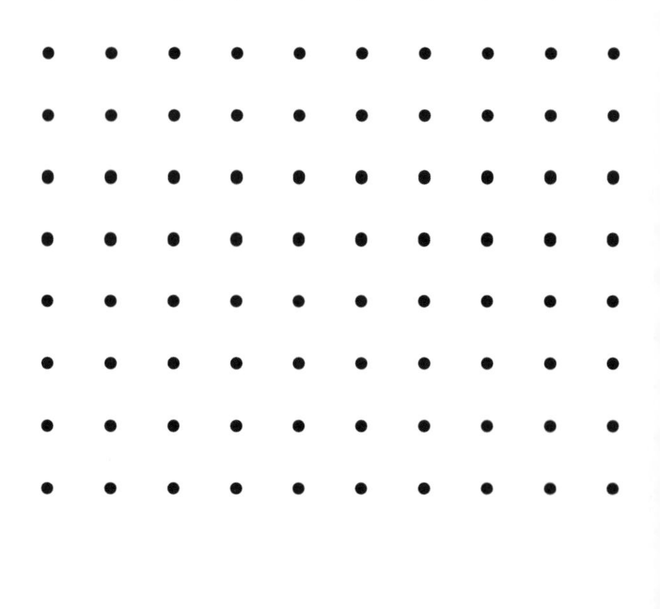

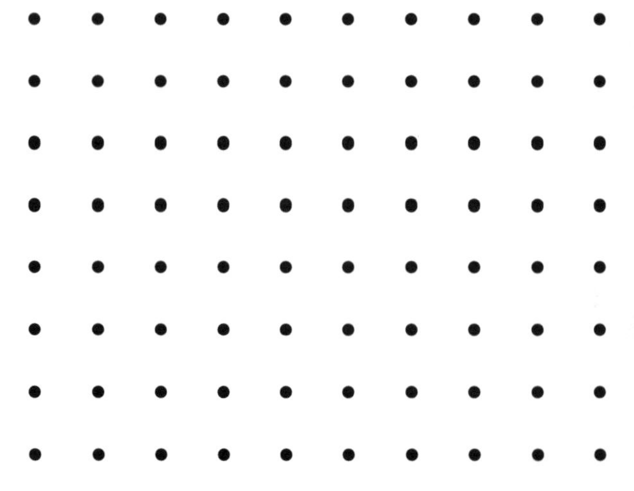

24

LEVEL MEDIUM

Copy each pattern to the grid beside it.
Begin with the marked dot.

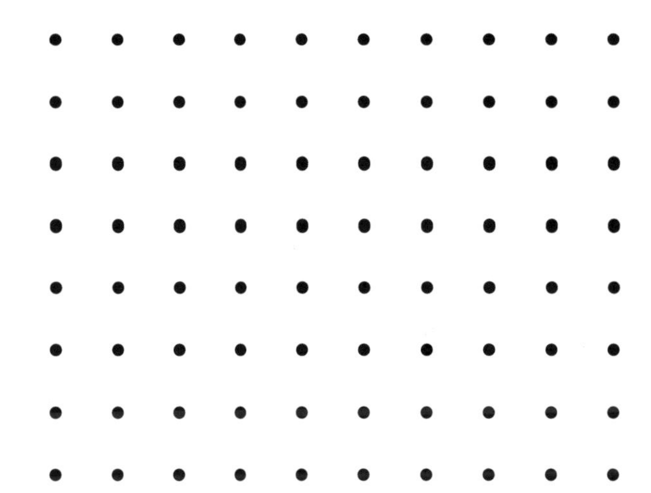

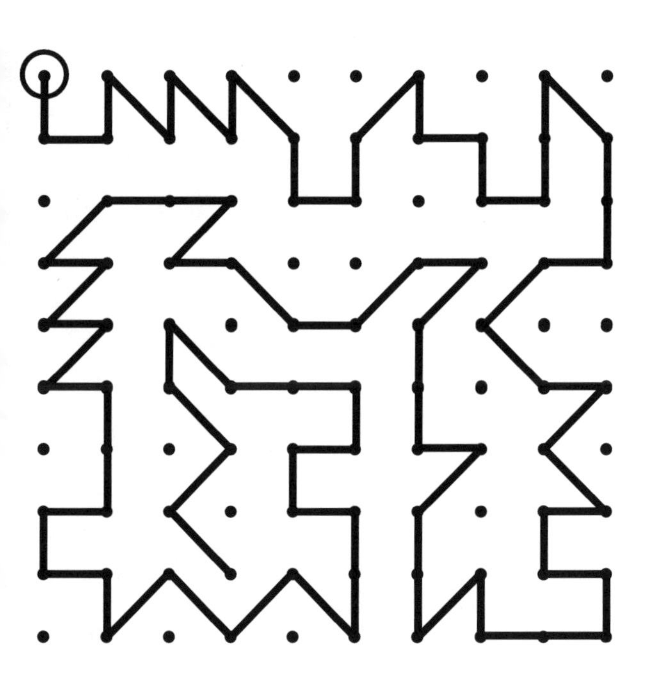

25

LEVEL HARD

Copy the pattern to the next page.
Begin with the marked dot.

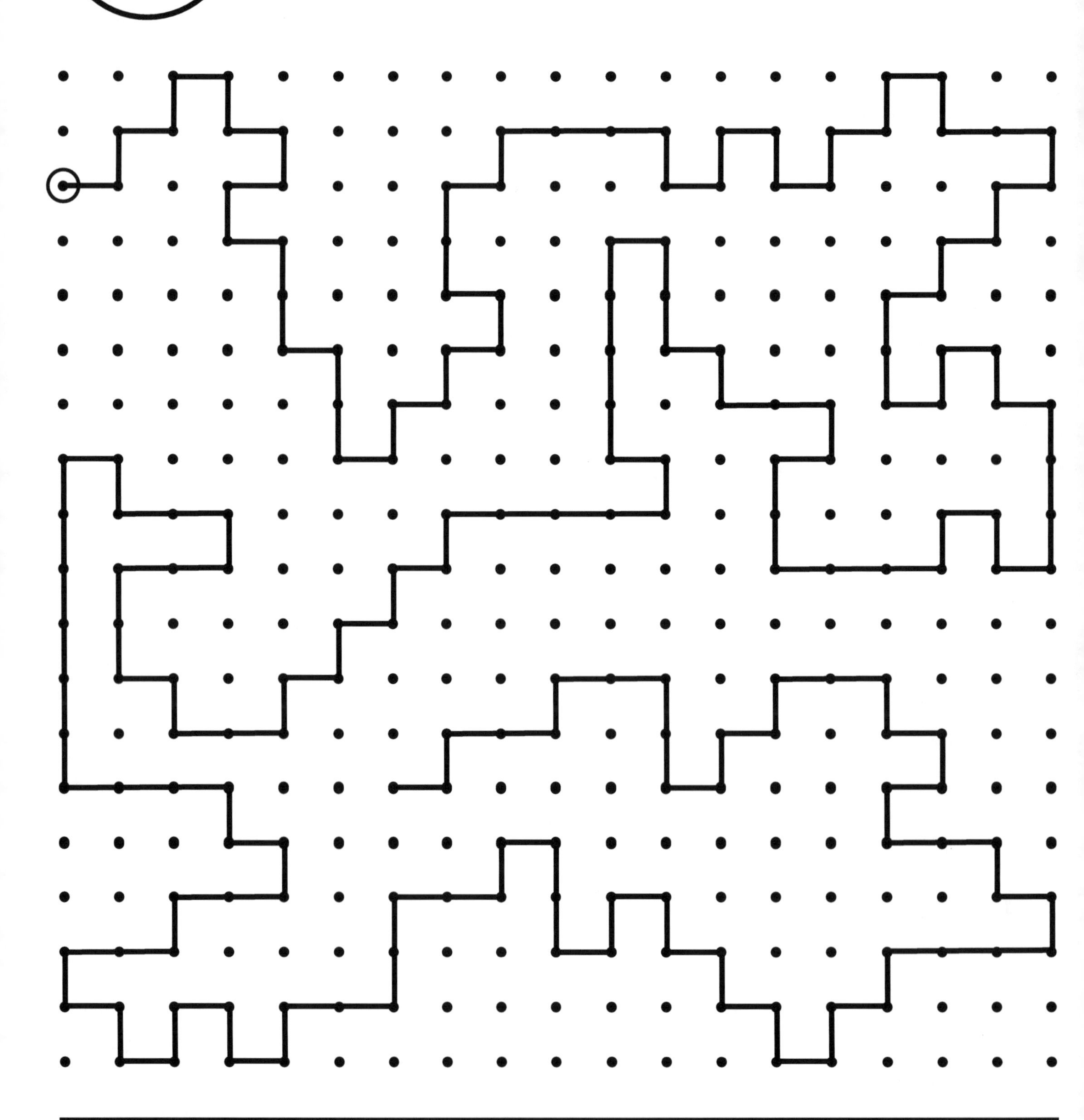

LEVEL HARD

26

LEVEL HARD

Copy the pattern to the next page.
Begin with the marked dot.

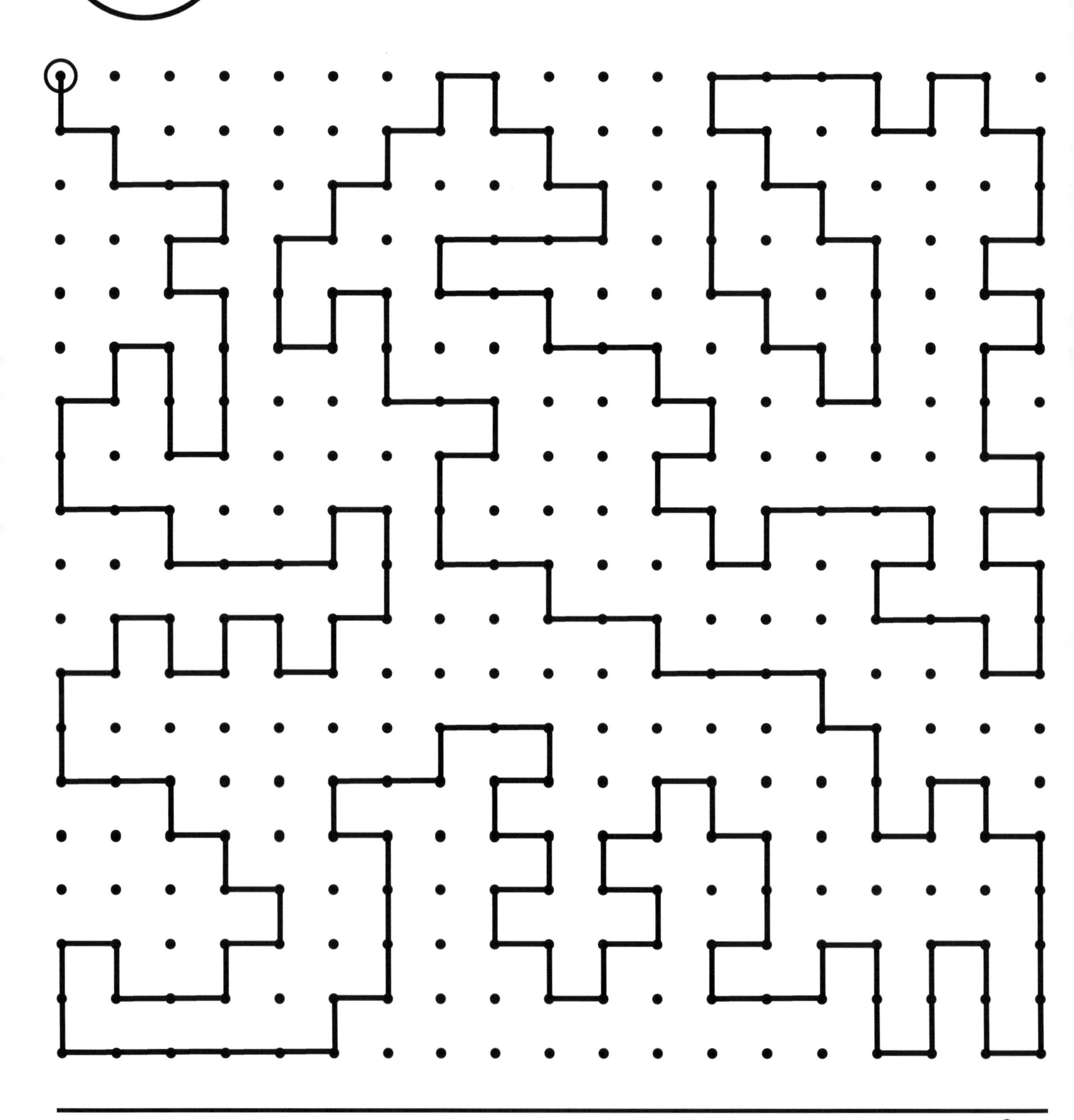

LEVEL HARD

TRACK AND COPY

Visual Treasure Chest

27

LEVEL HARD

Copy the pattern to the next page.
Begin with the marked dot.

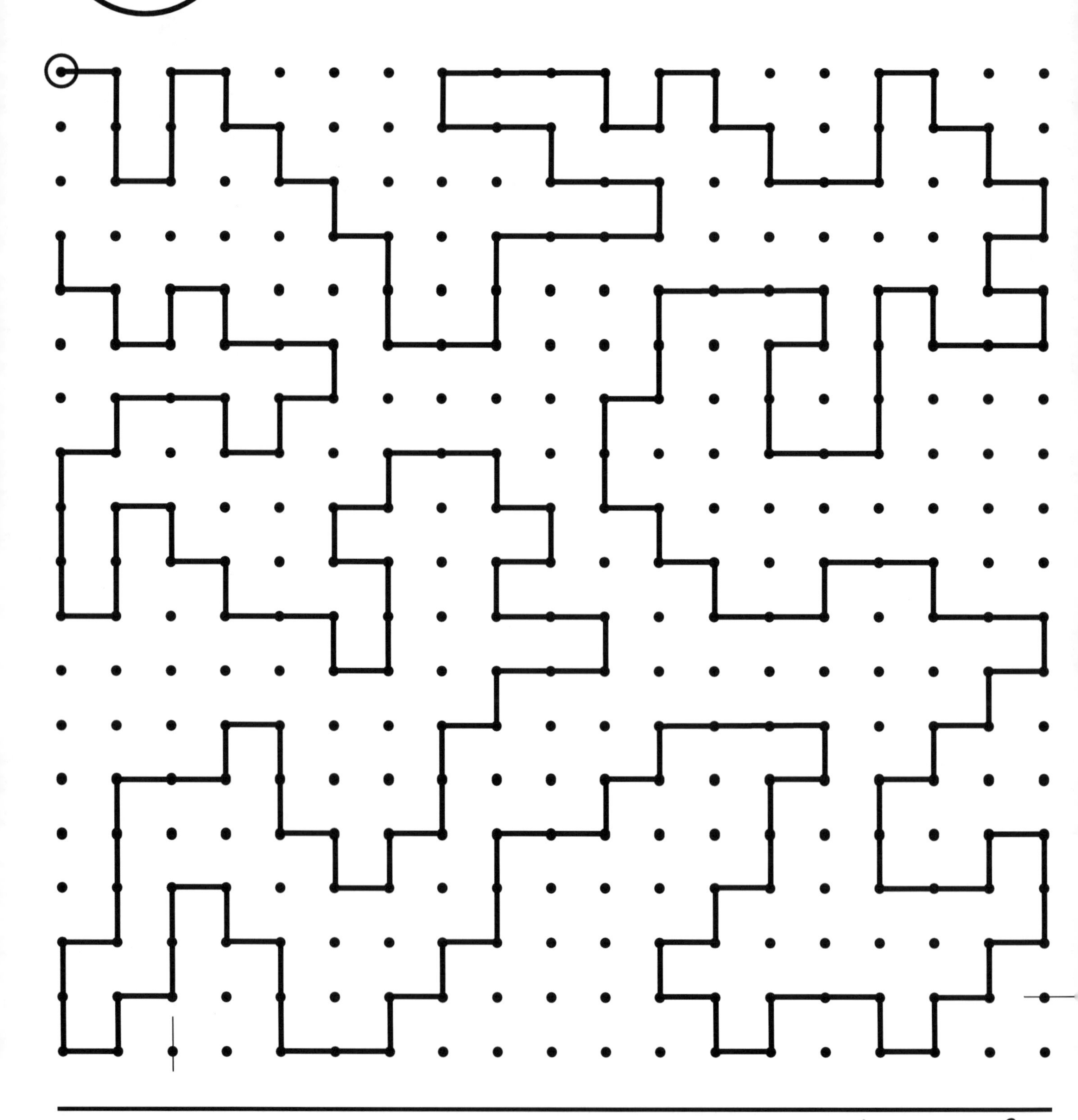

LEVEL HARD

28

LEVEL HARD

Copy the pattern to the next page.
Begin with the marked dot.

LEVEL HARD

29

LEVEL HARD

Copy the pattern to the next page.
Begin with the marked dot.

LEVEL HARD

LEVEL HARD

30

Copy the pattern to the next page.
Begin with the marked dot.

LEVEL HARD

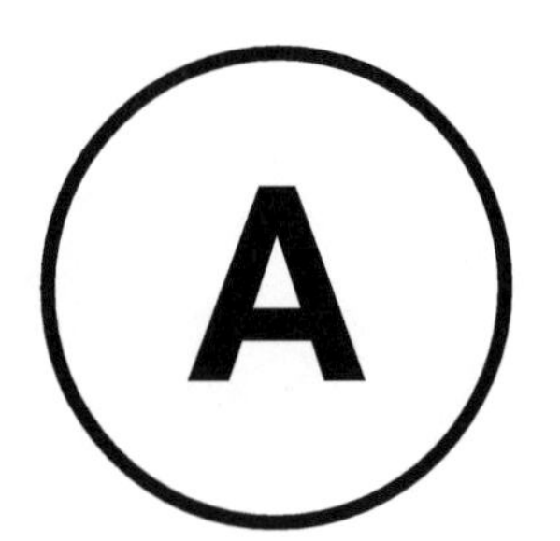

LEVEL EASY

Copy the patterns to the next page.
Begin with the marked dot.

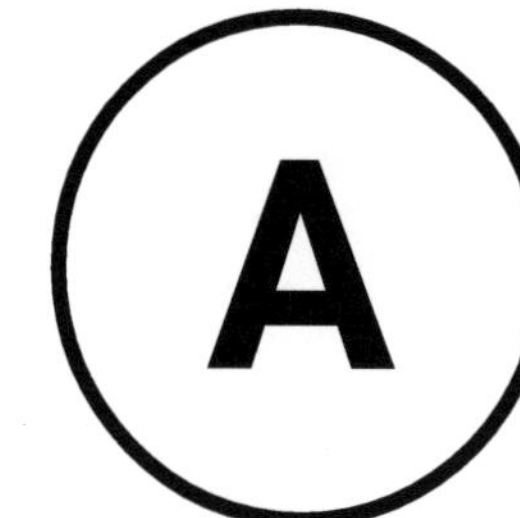

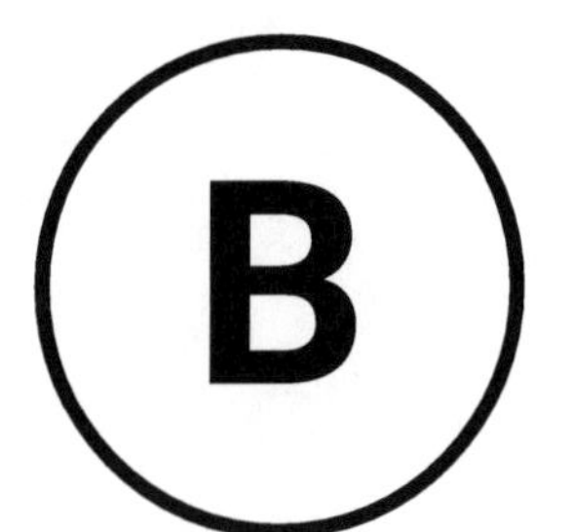

LEVEL EASY

Copy the patterns to the next page.
Begin with the marked dot.

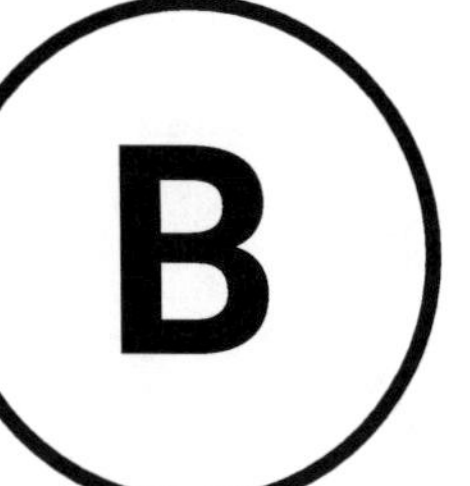

LEVEL EASY

TRACK AND COPY

C

LEVEL MEDIUM

Copy each pattern to the grid beside it.
Begin with the marked dot.

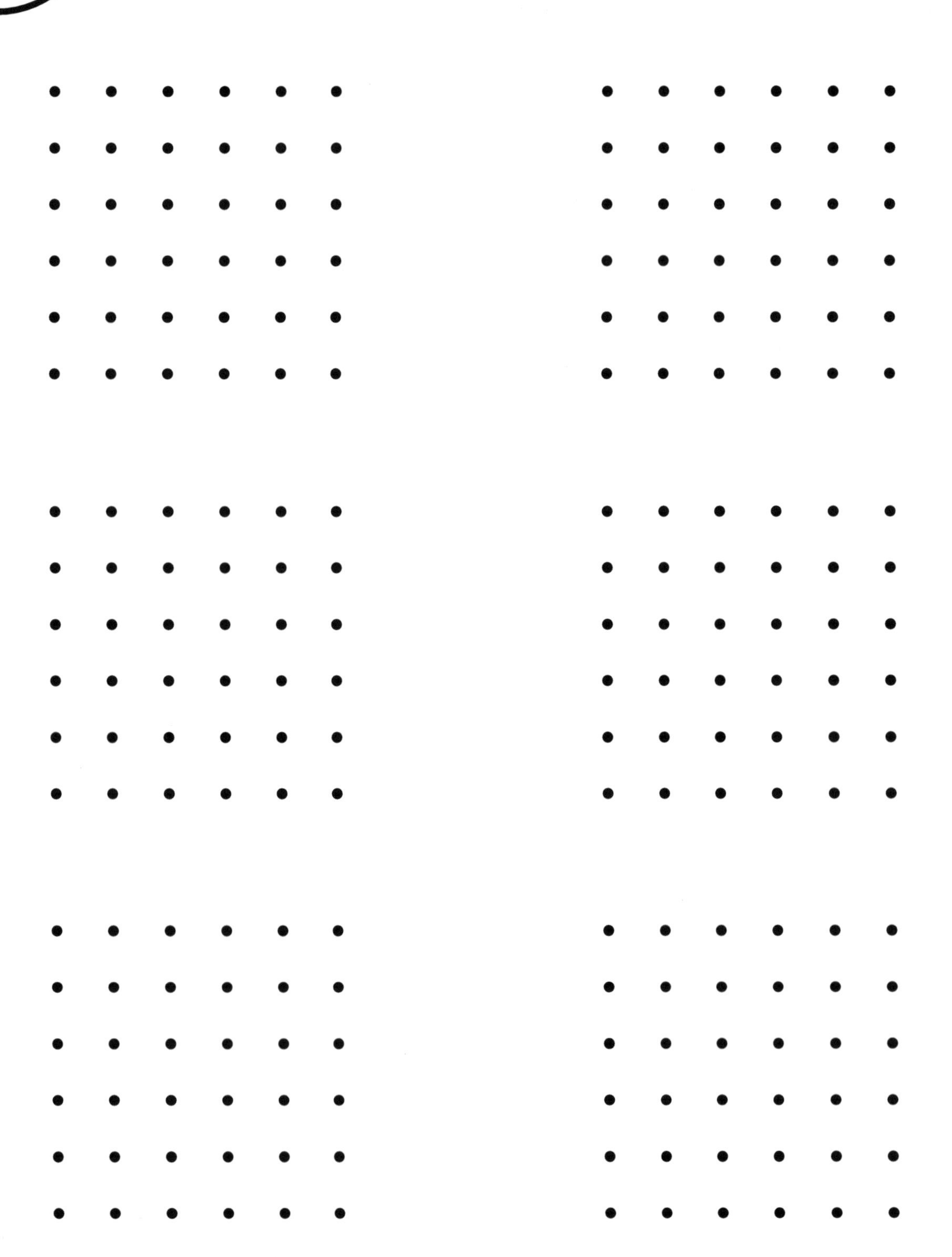

C

LEVEL MEDIUM

Copy each pattern to the grid beside it.
Begin with the marked dot.

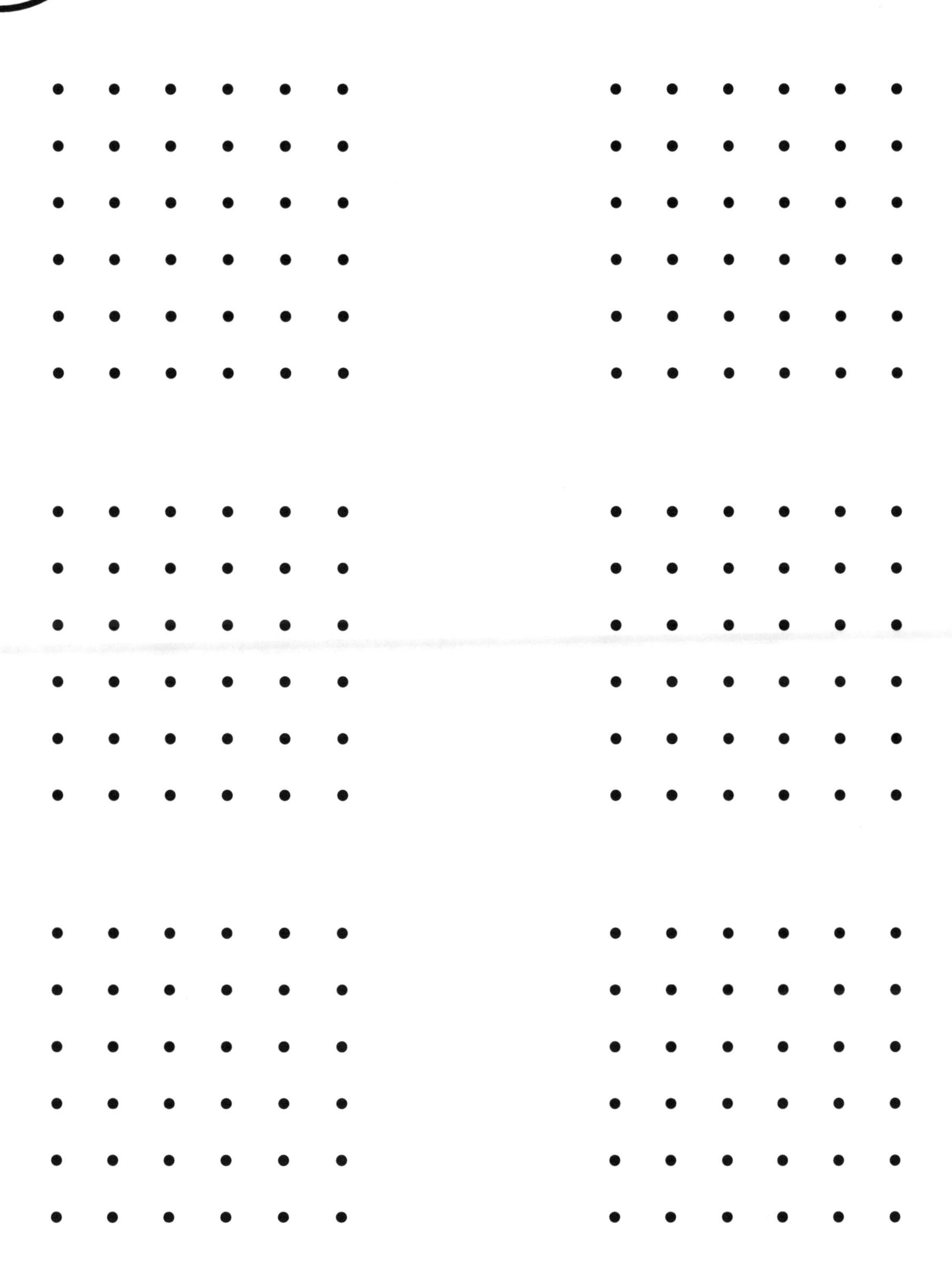

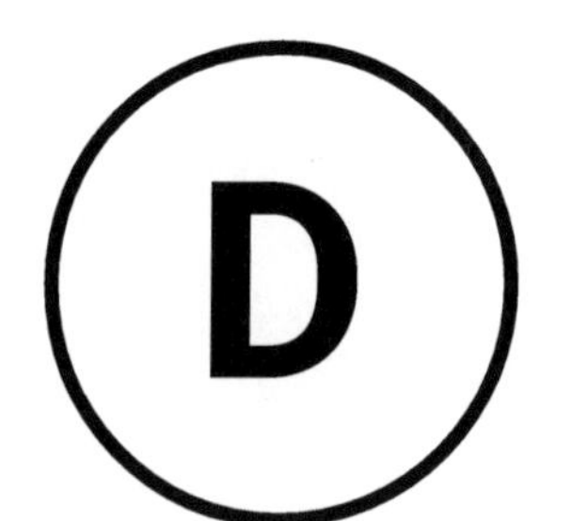

LEVEL MEDIUM

Copy each pattern to the grid beside it.
Begin with the marked dot.

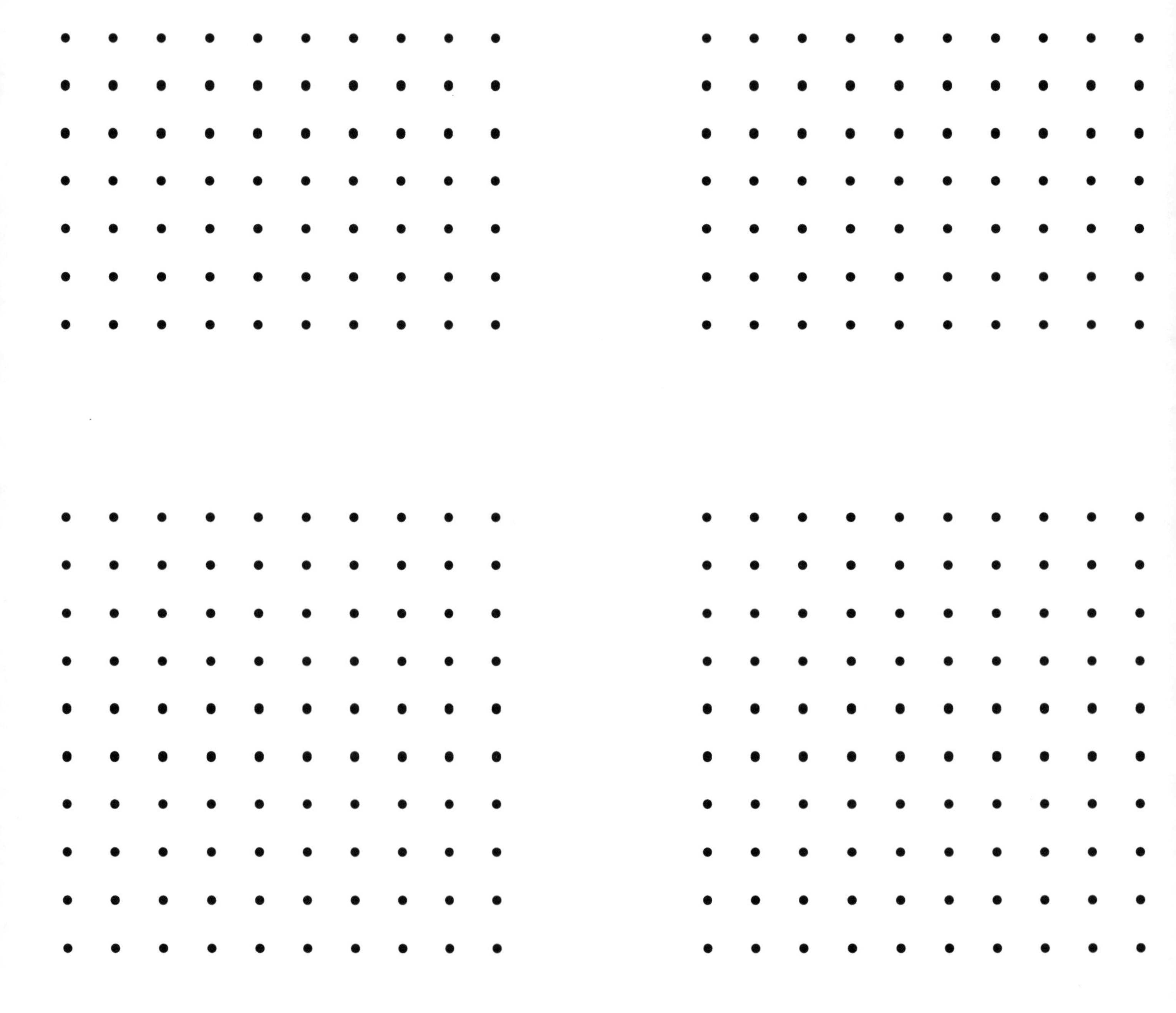

D

LEVEL MEDIUM

Copy each pattern to the grid beside it.
Begin with the marked dot.

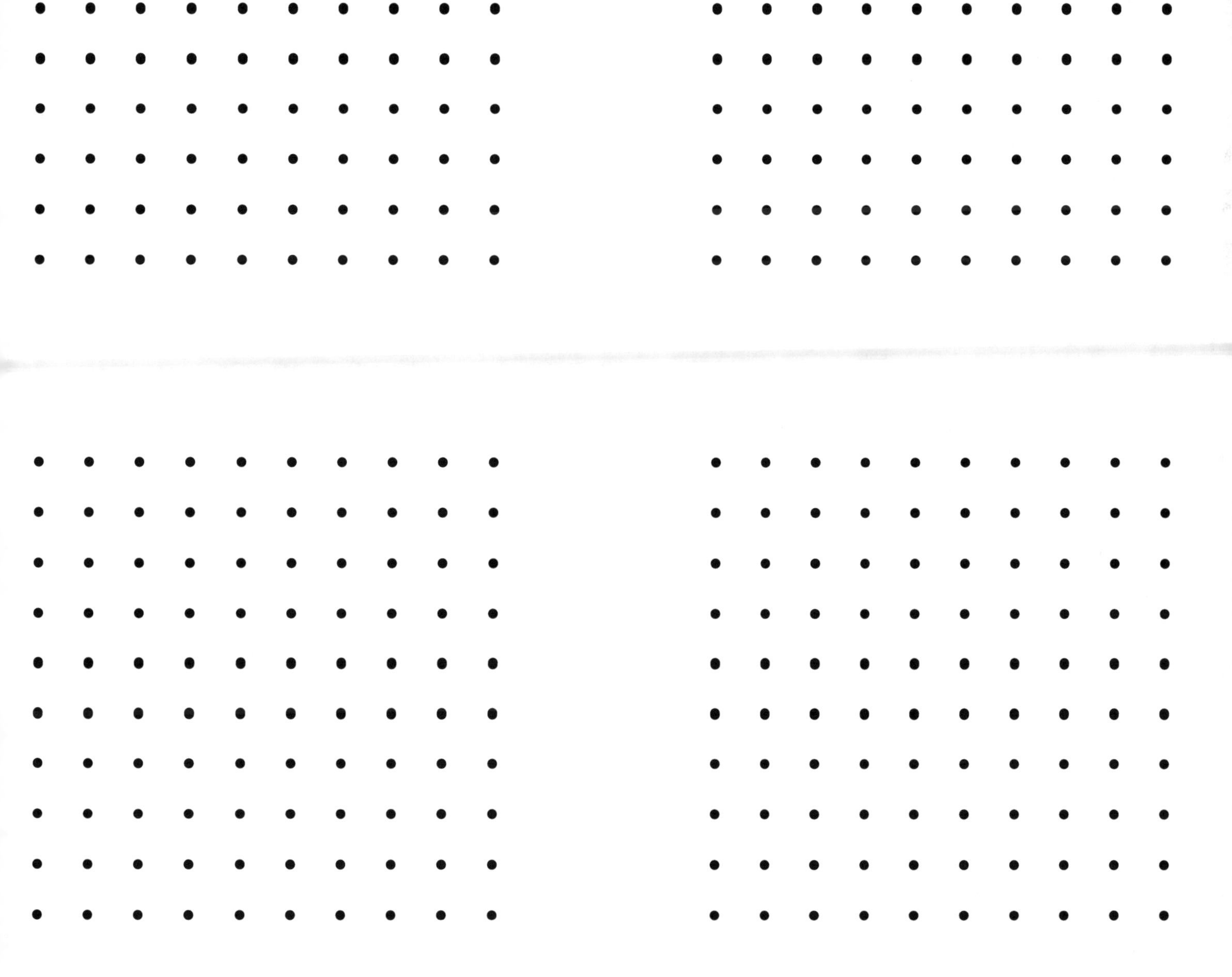

LEVEL HARD

Copy the pattern to the next page.
Begin with the marked dot.

LEVEL HARD

NOTES

NOTES

NOTES

THANK YOU
FOR PURCHASING THIS PRODUCT.

CHECK OUR OFFER ON
AMAZON.COM

*Visual
Treasure Chest*

Made in United States
Troutdale, OR
10/27/2023